## *About the cover -*

The portrait of the praying man on the front of this book is a photograph of a painting done by my father Clifton Bell.

This painting was Dad's last work prior to his unexpected death. Although he never acknowledged that it was his intent, it is obvious to his loved ones that the work is a self portrait.

Dad's heartfelt humility prevented him from putting his name on his work, but this painting was different. He was inspired to sign his *portrait of prayer*.

At the time he painted this picture Dad would have had no idea that his life on earth was soon to end. It seems that he was allowed to leave behind this priceless reminder that he was in prayerful contact with God prior to his death.

I believe that he was so moved by God's embrace that he felt compelled to share that comfort in the best way he knew - through his artist's brush with a God-honoring painting that expresses a message of hope to all who view it. For me, the signature represents his personal, intimate acknowledgement of the importance of prayer.

This painting and the message it portrays have become a personal healing tool for me in the wake of my own son's death. Every time I view the painting, I am reminded to pay attention to my dad's advice and go to my Heavenly Father for comfort.

# ~ *Acknowledgements* ~

•All Scripture quotations are taken from the Holy Bible, King James Version.

• Lyrics to *Small Graces* from the album, *Small Graces*/© 1997 Bright Avenue Songs/ Produced by Phil Naish for Naishing Teeth Productions/Co-produced by Ronnie Brookshire. *Words and music by Bob Bennett.* Reprinted by permission. All rights reserved.

• Lyrics to *Hand of Kindness* from the album *Small Graces*/© 1997 Bright Avenue Songs/Produced by Phil Naish for Naishing Teeth Productions/Co-produced by Ronnie Brookshire. *Words and music by Bob Bennett.* Reprinted by permission. All rights reserved.

• *What Noah Saw* from the book I'm Ready for My Rainbow, Lord by *Joy Morgan Davis*/©Joy Morgan Davis/Published by Fleming H. Revell a division of Baker Book House Company. Reprinted by permission. All rights reserved.

• Lyrics to *You Have Been Good* from the album *Bright Star Blue Sky/*produced by Spring Hill Music Group. *Words and music by Scott Krippayne and Tony Wood.* Reprinted by permission from Scott Krippayne. All rights reserved.

• *The Untroubled Heart* by *Paul Durham.* Reprinted by permission. All rights reserved.

• *The Blessing in the Thorn* by Don Koch/Dave Clark/Randy Phillips. ©1997 Word Music, Inc. (ASCAP), Definitive Music (Admin. by Dayspring Music, Inc.) (BMI), Dayspring Music, Inc. (BMI), Ariose Music, New Spring Music, First Verse Music (ASCAP) (Admin. by Brentwood-Benson Music Publishing, Inc.), World of Pentecost. All rights reserved. Used by permission.

• Excerpts from *Roses in December* by *Marilyn Willett Heavilin/* Published by Harvest House Publishers/©1987 by Marilyn Willett Heavilin. Reprinted by permission. All rights reserved.

• Graphic design for the photograph of the *white rose* was produced by *David Copeland.*

To Bri - Who loved our son unconditionally.
Buddies forever!

# Lifted up...
# ...from the Deep

## By Kim Simmons

**A - Corn Publishing**
**2002**

*Verily, verily, I say unto you. Except a corn of wheat fall into the ground and die, it abideth alone: but if it die, it bringeth forth much fruit.*

*John 12:24*

# Forward

Each chapter in this narrative is like one of many threads that have been interwoven throughout the tapestry God is creating in our lives. The stories in some chapters were sewn very abruptly at the time of our son's death. The threads of other chapters were set into the tapestry early on, but were knitted into place through the course of several years.

Oftentimes, as the knot is tied at the end of one chapter, the next thread takes us back to the beginning of the tapestry...where it all began on April 23, 1998.

As all of the chapters eventually intertwine with each other, it is the beauty of God's mercies that becomes a masterpiece.

---

### The Weaver

My life is but a weaving
Between my Lord and me,
I cannot choose the colors
He worketh steadily.

Oftimes He weaveth sorrow,
And I in foolish pride
Forget He sees the upper
And I, the underside.

Not till the loom is silent
And the shuttles cease to fly
Shall God unroll the canvas
And explain the reason why.

The dark threads are as needful
In the Weaver's skillful hand
As the threads of gold and silver
In the pattern He has planned

Author Unknown

# INTRODUCTION

As he looked up from the pages of the book, I sharply snapped at him. My selfish words rang through the air and I could hardly believe that I was criticizing him for spending too much time reading the Bible! After all, it was I who had been pushing to find a home church for our family. I had suggested that we were living in "perilous times." I felt it was time to get our "spiritual lives together." I had even expressed concern for the eternal welfare of our children.

Dave is truly a man of commitment. He will never do anything halfway. It's "all the way" or "not at all." After being married to him for nearly twenty-five years, I should not have been surprised to find him reading every page...one after another...night after night...until he fell asleep. I should have fully expected to find him in his chair early each morning with his coffee in one hand and his Bible in the other. It was becoming obvious that he was a "man on a mission." This part of the mission had begun in Genesis and would not end until the last page of Revelation was turned.

I had seen Dave's passion for reading many times before, but to read the entire Bible was going to take considerable time. I was finding myself angry about the hours he was spending in God's Word. It scared me to even consider being resentful about such a thing. (I wondered if my anger was stirred up by a sense of guilt that I spent too **little** time in biblical studies.) It seemed almost blasphemous to complain, but the words came out of my mouth.

Dave moved to the kitchen table and opened his Bible to a passage of scripture. He then told me that before he had begun his pilgrimage through the many pages of the Holy Book, he had asked God to guide and direct him. He had found himself worried for his family and was looking for guidance. He was looking for a "safe place" to lead his loved ones.

Dave then told me that several months earlier, after he had expressed these concerns to God, he had opened the Book in a random fashion and asked God to direct his eyes to the passage of scripture that would begin his journey to that "safe place." It seemed that Dave felt this passage might be his "personal message from God." He was not prepared for the verse that his eyes found.

Tears welled-up as he read the passage to me. He read from Micah

6:7......*"shall I give my firstborn for my transgression, the fruit of my body for the sin of my soul?"*

The words *"give my firstborn"* seemed to pierce Dave's heart like a thorn. I wondered if he was truly concerned that God wanted to prepare him for the possibility that something might happen to our oldest child, Jason. It was this verse that seemed to drive Dave to read and study God's Word with such determination and passion.

The very suggestion that something would happen to any of our children was more than I could bear. I quickly told Dave that any part of scripture taken out of context meant nothing to us personally. I told him that God doesn't work like that...(as if I would know how God might work in our lives!)

I quickly dismissed Dave's feelings as nonsense.

*"The name of the Lord is a strong tower:*
*The righteous runneth into it, and is safe."* Proverbs 18:10

As the head of our earthly family, Dave has become like a "tower of strength" because God has shown him how to become that. <u>God knew we would need a strong, Godly man in our future.</u> Dave's hours of biblical study laid the foundation for that crucial, spiritual growth.

Dave continues on through the pages of the Bible because he has discovered that studying God's word is a lifetime endeavor. He's not just reading page after page...he's savoring every word and is applying those words to our lives. Without a doubt, he has discovered the "safe place" for which he was searching.

Our family *is* truly safe and secure because we have each learned the name of our Lord...Jesus Christ, the Son of the Almighty God...the *"firstborn of every creature"* given for our transgression and for the sin of our souls.

As for **our firstborn son,** Jason...
he is the safest of us all...
**FOR HE IS NOW IN THE ARMS OF OUR LORD!**

*Lifted up from the Deep*

This is a story about our personal encounter with God.
It is humbly dedicated to the awesome glory of our Lord,
Jesus Christ.

It is written with deep love and appreciation
for the courage and compassion
shared by my husband,
Dave.

It is written in memory of our beloved son, Jason...
through whose death we see more clearly now.

*"For now we see through a glass, darkly; But then face to face: Now I know in part; But then shall I know as also I am known."*
**I Corinthians 13:12**

# Chapter 1

# The Perfect,
# Final Memory

Suppose you knew that any given day was the last day you would spend with a loved one. How would you spend it? What plans would you make to create that perfect, but final memory? What would be the most important details that you would want indelibly etched upon your mind?

So often I've heard it said, "Live every day as though it was your last." Suppose, however, that you had to "live *one* day as though it was your *loved one's* last to spend with you."

As inconceivable as it is to imagine, I believe I would try to fill the day with every positive emotion I could elicit - *love, joy, excitement, tenderness, pride.* If I could share all these passions one last time and could record them permanently in my mind, I would then have a beautiful remembrance of the most precious part of the one I loved...**his heart!**

## Easter Sunday
## April 12, 1998

I woke up early feeling exhilarated on that beautiful Sunday morning. It was wonderful to have all three of our "babies" at home with us. Ever since the boys had gone away to college, it was a rare occasion to have everyone home at the same time.

As the five of us began to get ready for church, I soon remembered days gone-by when mornings were always so hectic. Each other's "morning routines" always got in the way of another's space...only now the bodies were bigger and the shuffling around was louder. It wasn't until I heard the arguing about "bathroom time" or the pleas to find those "lost socks" that I realized just how much I had missed the "friendly fire" of those early morning interactions between our kids.

As I began to watch the clock, I thought about the last time we had all rushed around together to get to church on time. It seemed as though it was on a Sunday nearly three months earlier when the kids were each baptized. What a *blessing of comfort* it was to witness our children's public acknowledgement of faith that day. I looked forward to watching their individual, spiritual growth. I wondered how God would work in each of their lives.

Suddenly Jason came bolting down the stairs. He looked so handsome and was in his usual hurried state. I proudly straightened the knot in his tie and kissed him as he rushed out the door to pick up his fiancée Melissa and her grandmother. He and Melissa would sometimes attend services at her home church, but I had boldly insisted that they be with our family this particular Sunday.

I called to Wes and Jenny. Pride filled my heart as I watched them come down the stairs. We headed off to the Easter service where we were to meet my mom, my sister Leslie, and her family, Larry, Angie, Janice, Scott and Shawn.

As I took my seat, I gazed across the pew at my family. It was so wonderful to have everyone together. The only thing that could have perfected the morning would be if Dave's family had been there with us. I looked at Dave and noticed tears in his eyes. It touched me to see him so obviously moved and yet so peaceful. Dave is a man with a profound love for each of his children. He shares a special relationship with each of them - (Jason, his hunting buddy; Wes, his football protégé; and Jenny, his "little princess"). To share a love for Christ with his children would be the ultimate gift to Dave. This gift seemed apparent on this particular Sunday morning. Maybe that was what made this morning very special to him. Whatever it was, something was stirring deeply within his heart.

I then looked tearfully at my mom. She was a woman whose heart had been recently broken by the death of her son, my brother Chris. I was so glad she was with us on this day. I knew it was emotionally hard for her to be there. She was still raw with grief and the celebration of life-after-death through our savior's resurrection is always emotional. The fact that Jason was going to read a poem and that I was going to sing at the service would only add to her degree of sentiment. My mom always sheds a tear when I sing...not because I sing particularly well, but because that's what mothers do for their children...

...And that's exactly what I did for my child. As Jason approached the altar to share the poem he had been asked to recite, tears of pride welled up in my eyes. He had grown into such a wonderful young man. In just a few short months he would graduate from college. As he addressed the congregation with such ease and confidence, I could truly imagine him as a great teacher one day soon!

The song I chose to sing that morning was *"Watch the Lamb,"* by Ray

Botlz. I found it to be a very unique and moving approach to the crucifixion story. The lyrics powerfully describe what it may have been like to be in Jerusalem on that day. The story is told through the experiences of Simon of Cyrene - the man who carried Christ's cross to Golgotha.

I chose this song in particular because it expresses the *emotion* of the crucifixion. As I sang it, I imagined myself as if I was personally telling this story to my children alone. Our kids were "very young Christians" and I wanted them to think about the reality of what had actually happened at Calvary. I wanted to help them feel the importance of *coming to the foot of the cross with tears in their eyes* (a concept I had gleaned from a book by Max Lucado). That kind of passionate understanding cannot come from "book knowledge" or by "being religious." It can only come through real life experiences and through the "heart knowledge" that we are given. I prayed that my entire family, including myself, would deeply experience that awesome, personal knowledge throughout the course of our lives.

After church services we all met back at our house for an afternoon of eating and visiting. As we stood in a circle and held hands, we remembered the loved ones who were no longer with us and we gave thanks for the many blessings we had. Then the line quickly formed for food. We ate and laughed and shared stories. I smiled as I watched the kids share understanding tenderness with their Grandma Temp - a touch, a hug, a kiss.

The kids were especially anxious to get outside with Dave and Uncle Larry. Larry had brought a "potato gun" and that would prove to be the day's entertainment. The gun is like a bazooka. The ammunition is a potato stuffed down its barrel. Its trigger mechanism is a squirt of hair spray and a lighter. Uncle Larry's toy had very exciting prospects!

As the first potato flew through the air with a bang, I could hear cheers of approval from all the kids - including my 22-year-old. Jason was especially excited about the accuracy and "power" of the homemade gun. Above all the cheers I could distinctly hear him bellow **"awesome!"** Dave and Larry couldn't stuff potatoes down the barrel fast enough. Scott and Shawn (9-year-old twins) and our boys ("little boys" in huge bodies) took turns blowing potato after potato into the air. When the 20 pounds of potatoes were gone, the girls drove to town to buy more "ammunition."

They returned and told everyone that there were potatoes laying all over the highway (about a mile from our house). Jason believed their story without question and became even more excited. Of course the girls were only teasing about the potato-lined highway, but Jason's common sense and judgment were overshadowed by the level of fun and excitement he was having. I sometimes felt amazed at the degree of innocence and naívety my oldest son could display. I hoped that he might always be able to keep some of that innocence throughout his life. To me, it was precious. I often wished that I could capture some of his zest for life's little pleasures.

It was so wonderful to see my kids playing and laughing together. It was so refreshing to see them thoroughly enjoying each other as they shared this brief moment in time.

We all continued to share a wonderful day together until early evening. It was getting close to dark and my family needed to drive back to Kansas City. The boys needed to head back to college.

It had been a wonderful day of sharing
*love...joy...excitement...tenderness...*
And oh...
So much *pride*!

It was a day I would not soon forget!

**It was a day full of memories that will last a lifetime!**

*"...for your Father knoweth what things ye have need of,
Before ye ask Him."*
Psalms 6:8

*Lifted up from the deep*

# Chapter 2

# The Thorn

Tuesday April 21, 1998

It had been several days since our memorable Easter Sunday together. As the phone rang early on a Tuesday evening, I was happy to hear Jason's voice on the other end. He wanted to talk to his dad. I handed the phone to Dave and wondered what the discussion would be. Usually when Jay asked specifically for Dave it was regarding car troubles, hunting dilemmas or possibly money matters. As Dave hung up the phone, I heard him say "I love you, buddy."

Dave told me that Jason and Melissa had found an acreage for sale that they would like to purchase. Jay wondered if we would co-sign a loan for the land. Dave had calmly and caringly explained to Jason that such a purchase was premature. Jason was still in college. He had no idea where he might be employed after graduation. It was a big debt to be considering at this particular point in his life.

I could tell Dave felt bad that he needed to tell his son *no*, but neither of us could support such a move at this time in his life. Telling your kids *no* is part of being a responsible parent. I felt certain that Jason had matured enough at his age to understand our concerns. (He probably knew the answer before he ever asked the question!) I hoped that his disappointment in hearing *no* would pale in importance to hearing his dad's parting words, "I love you, buddy!"

Wednesday
April 22, 1998
*"boast not thyself of to morrow; for thou knowest not
What a day may bring forth."*
Proverbs 27:1

It was a beautiful spring morning. I wondered what the new day would bring...probably the usual "middle-of-the-week" routine...go to work...go to school...congregate back home for a quick dinner and a few laughs and a few phone calls.

Dave left for his long commute to Kansas City. Jenny left for her day of school and track practice. I left for work and a few daily errands. I looked forward to getting back home to enjoy working outside in the beautiful spring air.

This day seemed typical to us, but God had been planning it since the

*The Thorn*

beginning of time. He had every detail worked out before our eyes ever greeted the morning sun. Most times those details go unnoticed as we race through our frenzied lives. Sometimes, however, those details become *tender mercies* that we later cherish as gold.....

Dave received one of those *nuggets of gold* that afternoon as he drove home from work:

"**Hand of Kindness** - *the words were scrawled on a scrap of paper laying in the seat next to me. As I negotiated rush hour traffic on a sun-washed afternoon, my mind was so involved with gardening plans that I had forgotten to hit the 'drive-home-button' on the radio. For the first time in several years, my regular afternoon talk show accompaniment gave way to what my attentions considered 'elevator music.'*

"*Then I heard **that** song begin! The guitar work caught me and I turned up the volume. Before the song ended, I was in tears. I knew this was a song Kim would have to learn.*

"*I scratched the words on the first paper I could grab. I then focused on the 'thrust and parry' of rush hour traffic through the downtown loop. As the bottleneck gave way to suburban flow, my thoughts turned back to the evening's task at hand.*

"*The weatherman was predicting heavy rain for the weekend. I felt sure that it would be the beginning of a wet spring that could foil my chances to set up a garden for the season. The weather had been unusually dry and the soil was like powder. It was perfect for tilling if I could finish before the Friday afternoon deluge started!*

"*After I wheeled into the drive, I talked to Kim for a few minutes. I told her I had heard the next song she should learn and then I headed for the back lot. I dug until dark, downed a late dinner, and settled into the Lazy Boy.*"

**Told in Dave's Words**

*Lifted up from the deep*

**"Dad!...phone!..."** Jenny yelled down the stairs for her dad to pick up the phone.

As Dave answered that call, our lives changed forever. The journey immediately began down a road we never imagined we would have to travel.

The tone in Dave's voice was beyond description. Something was terribly wrong. I ran to the kitchen and just looked at him. He shook his head and asked, "Where were they?" It was at that point that I literally fell to my knees. I didn't know **what** to pray or for **whom** to pray. I couldn't even remember **how** to pray! All I knew was that I was driven to my knees and I instinctively knew that we were about to face a major storm in our lives.

Dave got off the phone and gave me the crushing news:

> Jason and Melissa had been in a head-on collision.
> The driver of the other car was dead at the scene.
> Melissa had been taken to a local hospital by ambulance.
> Jason had been life-flighted to a hospital in Kansas City.

Dave headed for the bedroom to change clothes. I ran upstairs to tell Jenny. She had been listening on the other end of the phone. I found her in her bed sobbing. She repeatedly cried, "...But, he's my brother...He's my brother..." Jenny quickly gained her composure and then grabbed a few things from her room before heading down the stairs:

> Dave called Wes...................*no answer*
> I called my mom...................*asked her to pray*
> Dave called the hospital........*Jay had not arrived yet*

I then scribbled down some important phone numbers.

**We headed for Kansas City for what felt like the longest drive of our lives!**

All I could think about and pray for during that agonizing ride to the hospital was that God would allow Jason to stay alive until we got there.

*The Thorn*

I didn't find myself praying that he would live, but rather that we could see him before he died.

Every once in a while, Dave would take a long, deep breath and then he would quietly utter the name of our Lord, "Oh, Sweet Jesus!" I asked him if he was okay. He calmly responded, "I'm just talking to God."

Jenny was curled up in the back seat, wrapped tightly in a blanket she had grabbed from her room. I reached back and took her hand.

I don't ever remember feeling so absolutely empty in my entire life. I felt like a shell...as if every bit of energy had suddenly been drained from me. I honestly could not get a grasp on what was actually happening to our family. I felt somehow protected from the smothering reality of what was about to occur in our lives.

For years I had prayed that I would stay close to God no matter what circumstances I might face in my life. I knew God would stay close to me, but I feared that my faith might falter if it was ever severely tested. When I would offer up these prayers, I honestly thought I was asking for help to face the tribulation of the world we lived in. My life had progressed so smoothly with very few "bumps in the road," but the world seemed to be growing colder with each passing day. I wanted to be prepared for any tribulation that would challenge me personally. I never expected to be facing a trial that would affect me so *intimately*!

I could hardly restrain myself from jumping out of the car before Dave had a chance to park in the hospital emergency entrance. My heart was racing. We ran to the emergency waiting room and found my mom, Leslie, Angie, and Janice. The girls were crying. I then saw the hospital chaplain talking to my family. It was then that the devastating reality of the situation quickly started to engulf every part of me.

I thought about how many times I had watched this very scene played-out on some television soap opera. This wasn't TV...this was *my* life! I didn't want to play a part in this real-life drama!

The chaplain seemed nervous as he tried to give us details. He asked if there was anyone he might call for us. We asked him to call our pastor. Pastor Dave is a strong, compassionate man who could bring us his much needed guidance and support.

My mind was reeling. I didn't know what to do or what to say. I glanced at my mom and noticed her hand trembling as she placed a cup of coffee on the table next to her. I glimpsed at the red, swollen eyes of my nieces. I turned and looked at my sister Leslie. She was trying to console all of us. She must have felt torn in so many directions as she comforted her own girls, our mother and my family. Who would console her?

A doctor came in and explained the injuries Jay had sustained. The list of problems was incomprehensible. Any one of these injuries, most notably a tear in his aorta, should have been life-ending. Only God's grace was holding our son until the proper time. I suddenly felt desperate to be by Jason's side. That was all I could think, "Let me be with my son so I can hold his hand!"

Dave called Wes - *still no answer!* - It was getting so late! Things seemed so imminent! It was crucial that we contact Wes!

My desperation grew stronger until the doctors finally okayed our presence in Jay's room. As Dave and I stood in the cold, sterile surroundings of the intensive care unit, I felt physically ill. Dave was also feeling apprehensive about going through those curtains into the cubicle where our son lay. We walked slowly together, arm-in-arm, to face the hard, bitter reality of what had physically happened to our beautiful son. The details will always be too painful to express and do not seem important to share. Suffice it to say that we held Jay's hand. We touched him. We prayed. We waited...

When Jenny came into the room she carefully placed her brother's hand on a small pillow that she had brought from home. It was her *good luck* pillow that she took to every volleyball game and track meet in which she participated. She seemed calm and peaceful as she lovingly stroked Jason's hand. Her strength brought me great comfort.

Dave seemed calm as he prayed aloud that "God's will be done." He allowed Jenny and me to share the one chair that had been placed at Jason's bedside. He watched as we both held Jason's hand. He understood a mother's need to nurture her son one last time and may have been sacrificing his own needs to touch his son for my sake.

Eventually, Dave got Wes on the phone. I don't know what he said to his son, but others who were present later shared their amazement at the strength and composure Dave was given as he told Wes the devastating news. Dave then called his mother, Marilyn, in Iowa and his

*The Thorn*

brother who lived about an hour away from Kansas City. Without hesitation, his mom and all his brothers headed to Kansas City in the middle of the night.

Pastor Dave had arrived. My mom had thought to contact Cindi, a precious friend of mine. She and another dear friend, Mary Ellen, were there for support. Now we could only pray that everyone would arrive safely from out-of-town and that Jason might live until that time. Dave later told me that he had specifically prayed that if his son was to die, that he not be just another statistic. He prayed that God would use Jay's death to glorify Himself.

The first prayer was answered as Wes walked hurriedly through the doors. His first question was, "Is he still alive?" I was overwhelmingly relieved to see him. I hugged him tightly as I told him that Jay was still alive. Wes then asked that he have some time alone with his brother.

When he emerged from the room he looked somewhat comforted. He then told me that he wanted Jason to have his college conference championship ring. That ring was probably Wes' most prized posses-sion at that time. He played football for the *Northwest Missouri State University Bearcats*. Wes lived and breathed football. He had shared time on the gridiron with Jay in high school. This gesture was so deeply heartfelt. I assured Wes that Jay would want him to keep the ring.

Then with big tears in his eyes, Wes told me that he and the Bearcats would win a national championship for Jason. I shuddered at the heartbreaking disappointment Wes would feel should such a goal not be realized. Wes never faltered from that promise.

Shortly thereafter, another prayer was answered as Dave's family arrived safely from out-of-town. We were in the corridor explaining the situation to them when a nurse came running out of intensive care and told us to come quickly.

> *"to every thing there is a season, and a time*
> *To every purpose under the heaven:*
> *A time to be born, and a time to die;..."*
> Ecclesiastes 3:1-2

God had purposefully planned every detail of this particular "season" in our lives. He had answered all of our prayers. In his infinite wisdom, he had answered some prayers *yes* and some prayers *no*:

Would God safely guide everyone to the
        hospital that night?......................................Yes
Would God's grace sustain Jason until we
        could all be by his side?.............................Yes
Would Jenny be allowed to share her love and
        adoration for her brother one more time?...Yes
Could Wes be blessed with a few last moments
        with his brother?.......................................Yes
Could I be allowed to just "be the mom" to my
        son one last time?......................................Yes
Would God give Dave the strength he needed as the
        head of this grief-stricken family?...............Yes

**Oh, dear God! Could Jason stay?!.........……...............No**

Every detail was in place...It was now time...**God's time!**

       *"Be still, and know that I am God...."*
                    Psalms 46:10

Everyone entered the room and stood silently.

As I held my son's hand one final time, I consciously savored every moment, studying the many features of his beautiful hand...every hair, every scar, every line. These were young, kind, hardworking, loving hands.

As I kissed his hand, I didn't even realize the moment of his death. The nurse started shutting down the monitors. I looked up and tearfully whispered, "Is he gone?" She shook her head. I reluctantly loosened my grip. Dave, Jenny, Wes and I all embraced. I fleetingly glanced up and wondered if Jason was observing this scene as he departed, now holding the hands of the angels.

*The Thorn*

The silence was suddenly broken by sobs of different family members. I looked over Dave's shoulder and saw our mothers embracing as they mourned the passing of their grandson.

Dave then walked over to Jay. He kissed him softly on the forehead and said, "I love you, buddy."

With that final kiss from his loving father on earth, Jason ascended into the arms of his loving Father in heaven........

**God's will was now done.**
**Would God be glorified in Jason's death?**

*That is the rest of our story...*

# Chapter 3

# Marks of Grief

I recently heard our pastor mention that we must sometimes become empty so that we might become filled. That truth describes the course of my life since that fateful night in 1998. I can still painfully remember what it felt like to become emptied and I now continue to humbly appreciate the assurance of how it feels to become filled with God's precious healing love.

My family had experienced God's incredible comfort months before Jay's accident when my brother died suddenly from a heart attack. God had placed a beautiful rainbow over the town of Pacific Grove, California, for the three days that we were there for Chris' funeral. The daily presence of God's gift was remarkable and so very uplifting. Even the semblance of a rainbow accompanied my family back home as sunlight found a prism through the windows of the plane. We each felt personally privileged to share in one of God's most splendid reminders of peace and hope.

I have since wondered if Chris' death somehow helped to prepare me for Jason's death. When I returned home from California I felt an urgency to passionately pray for my entire family. Chris' sudden death was an ever-present reminder of how fragile life can be. I pleaded with God to draw all of us closer to Him. I prayed that He would mend our broken hearts. I praised Him for his beautiful rainbow and asked His help in recognizing the many graces that are all around us. I begged Him that we would all continue to experience His comforting grace.

Four months later when another part of my world suddenly shattered, I was afraid that even God's grace could not possibly reach the depths of my sorrow. I feared that our family would never experience true joy again:

The hurt was too deep! The loss was too great!
The void was too profound!
***How would we each deal with such brokenness?!***

I can recall people telling me to "just keep busy." Keeping busy would "take my mind off of things." I didn't want to spend my life "keeping busy" in order to avoid thoughts of my son's death. The fact was that thoughts of Jason's absence were constant and all consuming.

*Marks of Grief*

There was absolutely nothing else on my mind or in my heart!

Other well-intentioned people suggested that "time would heal my wounds." I am still reluctant to believe that *time*, in and of itself, will **heal** anything. My wounds are no longer gaping holes and eventually only the scars will remain deep within my heart.

Scars are permanent marks that prove that wounds are, in fact, being healed. *Through* time, I have become convinced that my scar-laden heart is the sole result of God's healing touch.

> *"He healeth the broken in heart and bindeth up their wounds."*
> Psalms 147:3

God left these marks of grief on my heart to close those gaping holes that emptied my heart four years ago. My heart has actually become remolded as God has now filled that emptiness with His love. It's as though my heart has become more passionate about every emotion I experience....

I struggle against worldly pettiness that can fill one's life but I strive to notice and appreciate the simply majestic things that surround us daily.

I don't laugh as enthusiastically as before...but I cry much more easily.

I cringe at sarcastic, paltry words expressed by others, as well as by myself...but I get goosebumps with any gentle expressions of love that I observe.

I feel sorrowful for those I meet who fail to recognize the true blessings in their lives. I desperately want to reach out to people who may be suffering storms in their lives.

Amazingly, I worry less when my children are "on the road." I've learned that all the worrying in the world will not change anything.....but I pray tearfully and

*Lifted up from the deep*

constantly for strength to accept God's will...past ...present...and future.

I've learned what it means to come to *the foot of the cross with tears in my eyes*. This had been my prayer that Easter Sunday in 1998. God has brought us all to that solemn, sacred place and has responded to each of us in a perfect and personal way.

Reflecting further upon that Easter Sunday in 1998, I recall wondering how God might work in each of my children's lives. I now like to think that Jason was chosen as God's personal vessel to make our family more spiritually whole and healthy. That single thought truly keeps Jason more than just a memory. It keeps him an integral, connected part of our family. I could not be more proud of my son! My love for Jason, as with my other children, continues to grow deeper with each passing day.

It is an awesome thought beyond all comprehension that God intimately knows every person in His grand creation. Our family has been comforted and humbled with this truth time and time again since Jason died. Each of us has received *personally-designed gifts of healing*. In much the same way that God gives different spiritual gifts to the body of Christ to make all the parts whole, God has blessed our family with different healing gifts to make our family whole again.

God has tenderly knitted our broken hearts together, weaving a tapestry of family healing and bonding beyond measure. Our love for Jason is the common thread God has used to strengthen our family. In fact, I didn't realize until Jason's death that the biblical meaning for the name *Jason* is *"one who will heal."*

It's so very true that "the whole is stronger than the sum of its parts." Like the pieces of a puzzle as they all finally fit snugly together, the sum of everything God has done in our lives creates a truly magnificent picture.

# Chapter 4

# God's Moon

As we left the hospital and made our way back home on that daunting April night, Jenny broke the bleak, steely silence with a simple, but splendid statement of faith: "I'm jealous of Jason. He's the first of our family to see what heaven is like. He's the first to meet Jesus."

**Oh, how true scripture is!** As Jesus reminds us in the book of Matthew,

*"...out of the mouths of babes...thou has perfected praise;"*

Her praise did seem perfect. Her absolute certainty of Jason's eternal gift was praise in the purest form - trusting wholeheartedly in His loving kindness and His promised truth. Once again, Jenny's strength brought me great comfort.

It was nearly 4:30 in the morning when we finally turned onto the rock road to our house. On the eastern horizon emerged an incredible sight. As we wearily pulled into the driveway, we all got out of our cars and gazed at the great expanse of the eastern sky. A red hue shined from the waning moon as it lay just above the horizon. Two very distinct, large, bright "stars" seemed to hover above the moon. The lights were spectacular in the starkness of the country sky. In fact, the awesome display was the only visible thing in the otherwise void pre-dawn sky. Wes was the first to express what we all wondered...**"What is that in the sky?!"**

*"the heavens declare the glory of God,*
*And the firmament sheweth his handy work."*
Psalm 19:1

God's beautiful "handy work" that night will remain forever in my mind. In fact, whenever I see a crescent moon now, I find myself thinking about *April 23, 1998*. Was there a reason that this spectacular sight was ours to share as we returned home that night? Obviously, it was an astronomical occurrence that was not for our eyes alone...but it certainly felt as though it was placed "in the right place at the right time" for our wounded family to see. The beauty of that horizon felt like a blessing from God's heart to ours, comforting us as we entered our dark, empty house to face the painful reality that Jason would never be returning to this place we called home.

After just a few hours sleep, we got up to face the harsh reality of what had happened the night before. Somehow through the dazed backdrop of our anguish and confusion we "inadvertently" heard a news broadcast on the TV. Several people had called the station to inquire of the sight in the sky the night before. The reporter described the event as a "conjunction of the moon, Venus, and Jupiter." He reported that it was rare that the moon should pass between the earth and two planets at the same time. Such an event only happens about every 50 years. This celestial occurrence, involving Jupiter and Venus in particular, is even more rare...happening only every 500-1,000 years.

Initially, it was the *50-year-frequency* of the conjunction that most intrigued Dave. He immediately recalled the biblical importance of "the fiftieth year." According to Old Testament teachings, the fiftieth year was declared *a holy year of jubilee*. It was a time when slaves and servants were given their freedom and property was returned to its original owner. We found unexplained reassurance in the fact that our son was "set free and returned to his original owner" on the night of God's 50-year sign in the sky.

What may seem to be a very simplistic explanation of such a glorious event in the sky was the exact degree of understanding that we needed. It was all we could grasp at such a fragile time in our storm. Although it was only a "small pearl of wisdom," it became a priceless reminder of the truth of our circumstance:

*It was Jason who had actually "returned home" the night before. We were the ones who would someday join him "at home."*

I remember when Jason left for college in 1994, I had written to him that each night while he was away, I would look at the stars and remind myself that they were the very same stars that he could see. I told him to look at the stars every night because I would pick out one in particular and call it his...and then I would throw him a kiss goodnight.

The brightest star in the conjunction we saw the night that Jason went home was Venus, *the morning star*. The Bible describes Jesus as the bright and morning star. Now, almost every night I look for Venus in the nighttime sky. As I blow Jay a kiss, I wonder if he could be looking at the same star from a wondrous, new vantage point.

How the light from the planet Venus must pale in comparison to the brilliance he sees in the face of the true "bright and morning star!" I cannot comprehend the incredible beauty he must be experiencing as he gazes across the great expanse of God's universe from beyond the moon and stars that I can see:

*"but it is written, eye hath not seen, nor ear heard,*
*Neither have entered into the heart of man,*
*The things which God hath prepared for them that love him."*
1 Corinthians 2:9

*God's Moon*

"When I consider thy heavens,
The work of thy fingers, the moon and the stars,
Which thou hast ordained;"   PSALM 8:3

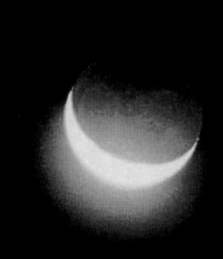

**Photo taken by Marco De Bellis
Rio de Janeiro (Brazil)
April 23, 1998**

*Lifted up from the deep*

## A note about the photograph

The photograph we used which so brilliantly portrays the conjunction was found on the Internet. After many months of searching, we found pictures of the event, but none truly illustrated what we saw that night. We knew it would be unlikely that we might find a picture showing the same alignment of the moon and planets as we remembered them. To accomplish that, we would have to find a picture that was taken at the same time of the night as our viewing. The odds were great, but Dave set out one particular night in one more earnest attempt to find it.

It was well after midnight when Dave woke me up. "I've found the picture you've been looking for. It was taken in Brazil!" I jumped up from my sleep, looked at the photograph and immediately knew that this was it - the perfect picture!

I was elated! I showed it to anyone who would take the time to appreciate its splendor. For weeks I would gaze at it and think passionately about my son. I felt wonderfully blessed that we had found this *precious work of art*. It so powerfully illustrated God's *perfect work of art*. My biggest concern was if the photographer, Marco De Bellis, would allow me to publish it in a book. I was reluctant to write to him. I didn't want to face any possible rejection of my request, especially after feeling so privileged to have even discovered the picture.

On **Sunday, April 1, 2001,** I felt compelled to go to the computer and send the request. I had been putting it off for some time and felt as though this was the day that I needed to follow through. I wrote my thoughts to Marco De Bellis, took a deep breath, and pushed the *send now* button. As my message disappeared from the screen and travelled on through "cyberspace" to Rio de Janeiro, I prayed that the artist would receive my petition with an open heart:

April 1, 2001

Dear Marco De Bellis,

I am writing with great appreciation for your picture of April 23, 1998, of the conjunction of the moon, Venus and Jupiter. It is absolutely incredible and of particular significance to me and my family.

That particular night in 1998, our son died in an automobile accident. As we were returning home from the hospital, we were almost "startled" to see this beautiful sight in the sky. It brought us much needed comfort at a very devastating time in our lives.

Your photograph depicts exactly what we remember seeing on that daunting night in April. I am in the process of writing a book regarding the experiences we have had surrounding our son's death. Should this book ever be published, I would like to use your photograph of the conjunction. Your picture shows what I have not been able to describe to others. I am writing for information in regard to the possible use of this photograph for this type of project.

Again, I cannot begin to tell you what our discovery of this picture has meant to me and my family. We had searched for months before we found the photograph that captured what we saw that night. It must have been taken at about the same time we saw the event in the sky. Thank you for your time and consideration.

Sincerely, Kim Simmons

The next day as I wrote my "final thoughts" regarding the conjunction of April 23, I placed a blank sheet of paper between the pages where I hoped to someday place the photograph. As I stared at the blank page, I wondered if my mail had been received. I decided to quickly check our email before shutting down the computer. Much to my surprise, Marco De Bellis had, in fact, already responded. It was with nervous apprehension and hesitation that I downloaded his letter.

I was overcome with tears as I read the beautiful response.

---

Dear Dave and Kim,

It was with great emotion that I read your message concerning my photograph of the conjunction of April 23, 1998. The message was dated April 1st. On April 1st, 1995, I also had a very devastating time in my life. I lost a 20 year old son in an automobile accident.

Only those who have suffered such a thing can evaluate the meaning of it.

I can hardly believe the date of your message and that the above-mentioned are only a simple coincidence. It sounded as a message of comfort came from God.

Regarding the photograph, it is yours; feel free to use it to illustrate your book....

...just for curiosity, I would like to know how did you find the image? It can be found in only one place in the web.

Finally, I could not hide my desire to read your book, when finished.

Your brother,

Marco Antonio De Bellis

---

In the great vastness of this world, I am awestruck that God will remember the smallest details of individual lives, mold those details together at just the right time, and create a perfect gift.....just to prove His love for us.

Only God could bring two families together from different parts of the world to share such unexpected joy. At a perfect moment in time, total strangers shared incredible comfort that was the result of a shared understanding of each other's incredible grief. He truly "makes all things beautiful in His time." He is always faithful!

I was speechless! That great hymn written by Thomas Chisholm describes my emotions completely:

### *Great Is Thy Faithfulness*

*Summer and winter, and springtime and harvest*
*Sun, moon and stars in their courses above*
*Join with all nature in manifold witness*
*To Thy great faithfulness, mercy and love*

*Great is Thy faithfulness!*
*Great is Thy faithfulness!*
*Morning by morning new mercies I see*
*All I have needed, Thy hand hath provided*

### *Great is Thy faithfulness, Lord, unto me!*

As time went on, the "small pearl of wisdom" that we were given about the conjunction of April 23, 1998, grew into a much deeper awareness of God's great signs in the sky. Dave continued a journey of study he had begun nearly a year earlier about the subject of biblical astronomy:

> "As I heard the newscast regarding the predawn conjunction, I remembered several things I had studied regarding God's literal revealing of the gospel in the heavens. The fact that Venus and Jupiter were the

*Lifted up from the deep*

planets involved in this particular event sparked my attention.

"About a year earlier, I had heard a man discuss biblical <u>astronomy</u> (not to be confused with <u>astrology</u>). His premise is that since the creation God displayed His plan of salvation through stories told in the constellations."

---

*"And God said, let there be lights*
*in the firmament of heaven*
*To divide the day from the night;*
*And let them be for signs, and for*
*seasons, and days and years."*
Genesis 1: 14-15

God has set these lights in the sky
for signs.
**What do the signs mean?**

---

"The message in the stars is not about our love life, as astrology suggests. Rather the message may well be about <u>God's love</u> for us and our redemption from this broken world. Through the ages, the original themes of the constellations have become corrupted and distorted. The truth, however, is told in the Bible: *'**He** calleth them all by their names'* (Psalm 147:4). The Bible further indicates that as long ago as when the <u>Book of Job</u> was written, the constellations were studied. The author of Job writes about the constellations and calls them by name, *'Arcturus, Orion, Pleidis, the Chambers of the South'*. (Job 9:9)

"Several Christian writers have provided evidence of God's original record as placed in the pictures portrayed by the stars, (James Kennedy, William Banks, E.W. Bullinger, Joseph Seis).

" A few examples of the names that God gave the constellations are :

**Virgo** the Virgin *('behold, a virgin shall conceive, and bear a son.'* Isaiah 7:14)

**Aries** the Lamb *('behold the Lamb of God, which taketh away the sin of the world'* John 1:29)

**Leo** the Lion *('behold the lion of the tribe of Judah, the root of David'* Revelation 5:5)

**Hydra** the Serpent *('and the Lord God said unto the serpent- upon thy belly shalt thou go'* Genesis 3:14)

"On the day after witnessing the conjunction, I remembered that the **planet Jupiter** is said to be representative of God (the Hebrew word for the planet we call Jupiter means righteousness).

"The planet Venus is called the bright morning star (a name used in the Bible for Jesus Christ). From a perspective on Jupiter facing the earth, Venus would be on the right hand side:

> *'so then after the Lord had spoken unto them,*
> *He was received up into heaven,*
> *And sat on the right hand of God.'*
> Mark 16:19

"Just as the moon's only light is reflected from the **sun** (the source of light of our physical world), we are told to be a reflection of the **Son** (the source of light of our spiritual world.)

*Lifted up from the deep*

"The moon was lying on it's back in the position
of a slightly tipped cup....
"The planet Venus was on Jupiter's right...
"The planet Jupiter was the highest object in the sky..

"As we looked into the eastern sky with the agony of the night's events tearing at our hearts, we were confronted with a celestial snapshot of our compassionate Father's love.

"In this darkest hour, we saw a depiction of Christ sitting on the right hand of our most high Father. His light was pouring into the cup-shaped moon, overflowing into our world of darkness - on the night our beloved Jason was set free and returned to his rightful owner."

Thank you, Lord Jesus
Amen

(As told in Dave's words)

**I pray that we might become a brighter reflection of his love
With each passing day.**

*God's Moon*

# Chapter 5

# God's Dove

In the midst of the confusion and despair of the morning after Jason's accident, we received a phone call from my sister Leslie. That phone call helped us to face the day's overwhelming tasks-at-hand. Her news gave us the strength to move forward with the many phone calls we had to make and the countless, unbearable decisions we had to confront.

Quite frankly, at a time when I could have doubted if God still loved us, we received assurance that He loved us profoundly. Leslie told me that our mom had looked out her kitchen door that morning to discover a white dove nesting in an old plant basket on her deck.

**A white dove?!  Was she sure?!**
**I had never seen a real white dove in my entire life!**

Life is sometimes very hard and uncompromising...but God is so majestically good! What a blessing it was to hear that He had sent this *bird of comfort* to my mother. I had been praying that my mom would experience God's personal presence in her life ever since my brother died. This seemed like an answered prayer, but the circumstances surrounding that answered prayer were so painful!

My mom first noticed the dove on the morning that Jason died. I asked her daily if the dove was still there. She would assure me daily that it was still nesting on her deck. The simple knowledge of the dove's presence helped soothe the pain of those early, agonizing days.

The dove stayed for the three days before Jason's funeral.
It flew away on the day of the funeral.
Mom never saw the dove again.

We had gone to Mom's house several days later and I could hardly wait to see and touch the nest. Dave brought the priceless reminder of God's gift inside. The fragile nest cradled a tiny egg. Dave carefully removed the egg, held it in his hands and adoringly explained that "the dove had left her own testimony." We asked Mom if we might take the egg and nest home with us.

Although it seemed like a lack of faith on my part, I started to research the characteristics of doves. I was afraid that some people would not

*God's Dove*

believe the beautiful truth that a white dove appeared at my mom's house and then abruptly left as quickly as it had come. Mom assured me that the bird was pure white. The nest and the size and color of the egg perfectly matched the description I studied.

We placed our priceless treasure in a glass container so that we might always remember the grace and mercy God sent to us in our greatest hour of need. As pastor Dave had mentioned at Jason's funeral, the white dove is symbolic of God's Holy Spirit. In addition to that comforting thought, we found consolation in the recognition that an egg represents "new life." Our most cherished hope for Jason is that he has been blessed with "new life" in God's compassionate care.

God's ways are not our ways. I strive so often to understand why things happen as they do. Through my imperfect way of trying to appreciate God's plan for our lives, I pray forgiveness for any presumptions I might make in my meager understanding of things. As I continue to marvel God's placement of the dove, I ponder His mysterious ways. It occurred to me recently, for example, that when my mom lost her precious son, I was given a gift of spiritual growth and preparation. When I lost my beloved son four months later, my mom received a miraculous gift of healing that would undoubtedly touch her heart forever. We were both blessed in the wake of such sorrow:

> *"and we know that all things work together*
> *For good to them that love God, to them who*
> *Are called according to his purpose."*
>
> Romans 8:28

I feel as though Chris and Jason were both "called according to His purpose." Their deaths have worked together for good....

> God's ways are **not** our ways,
> But God's ways **are** good!

It seems important that we not consider every "unusual" occurrence in our lives as having profound, spiritual significance. It is **God's** will to give signs and wonders. It may be that we sometimes allow **our** will to mistakenly construe some things as *signs from God.* To become flippant in our interpretation of things, however, diminishes the truth of the sovereignty of God's choices for our lives.

On the other hand, how often does God offer us tender mercies that we choose to ignore as gifts from Him? By our own will, we may define happenings in our lives as "mere coincidences" or as "just plain weird." Is it possible that we are an affront to God when we fail to acknowledge the special gifts that He does, in fact, give us?

### **It is with these concerns that we constantly pray for understanding.**

Dealing with Jason's death has brought many waves of emotion. The ebb and flow of anguish we feel from the loss of our son  is like an emotional roller coaster ride.

Many months after Jay's death, when I was journeying through one of those downhill sides of this emotional ride, I was standing on our front porch wondering if the ache would ever leave my heart. I glanced through a window at the glass container which held our dove egg. It was evening and the lamp next to the container was on. As I studied the nest and egg, I suddenly realized that there was a beautiful reflection in the glass. I told Dave to come quickly and look closely at the glass jar. I asked him what he saw.  He confirmed that the reflection looked like a dove hovering above the egg!
I was flooded with peace and encouragement as I gazed at the image.

**The glass had *always* been in that exact spot.**
**The light had *always* been in that precise place.**

In God's perfect order of things, a reflection was naturally created...but this reflection seemed "custom-made."

Although this reflection had obviously been in place since we put the glass container in that location, God directed my eyes to it at a time when I needed a large dose of His spiritual nourishment:

*God's Dove*

*Small graces surely have a meaning.*
*Beyond their merely passing by,*
*They are a reminder to the heart.*
*There's more to life than meets the eye*
From the song *Small Graces*, by Bob Bennett

Sometimes what seem like mundane choices in our lives are actually decisions that result in a masterpiece. Dave had chosen the round jar to hold the egg. I had chosen to place it by a lamp that happened to have a white base and a dark, square shade. All of those combined choices created the perfect reflection.......

..........maybe our lives are a bit like that. Suppose those everyday choices we make in our lives are really instruments of growth that, when guided by the Master's hand, become a beautiful masterpiece - *a reflection of Himself!*

**Just imagine the joy we will feel when we finally get**
**To see the finished portrait!**

*Lifted up from the deep*

# Chapter 6

# God's Song

Early on, one of the many decisions that had to be made quickly was the choice of music to be played at the funeral. Dave and I both wanted the funeral to be our own personal last tribute to our wonderful son. He deserved the best we could offer. No one is ever prepared to know how to plan such a service, but we knew that the music had to be special. How could we make such a decision when it was nearly impossible to truly focus on anything?

Dave suddenly remembered the *nugget of gold* he had been given on that drive home the night of the accident. He felt an urgency to find the song he had heard on the radio that evening. He went to his truck and found the scrap of paper where he had written the title of the song. Scrawled on the paper were the words *"Hand of Kindness."*

That's all we knew - those simple words *"Hand of Kindness."* We didn't know the artist's name or the album from which the song was released. One thing we did know for certain, however, was the burning desire in Dave's heart to find the song. My dear friend Nance dropped everything immediately and promised she would find the recording. There was not a doubt in my mind about that! What a precious gift such a friend is from God! What a beloved gift she became **to** God when she so willingly allowed Him to use her hands and heart to accomplish His will for us.

The tape arrived within hours of our request. Dave, Wes, Jenny and I went into our bedroom and sat together behind closed doors to listen carefully to the words of the song. We cried as we listened to the beautifully-perfect lyrics. This was the song that would be played at Jay's service. God had chosen this song for us and had given it to Dave before we even knew why.

I personally found that one of the hardest things to initially accept was the fact that our son had to experience the most profound event of his life without our presence. We had always been there to support him as he journeyed through life. We could not be there to walk "through the valley" with him. That thought was devastating to me as a mother. I thought of him as my young and rather naïve son who was making a final journey by himself. For me, the song was a wonderful reassurance that he was **not** alone...he was being guided by the truest *hand of kindness*.

As I listened to the song, I actually found myself imagining that it was

Jason reassuring us that he was truly okay. Even though he was a "young Christian" with a new understanding of the importance of having a Savior, he understood that he does, indeed, have a Savior.

## Hand of Kindness
### By Bob Bennett

I've no need to be reminded
Of all my failures and my sins
For I can write my own indictment
Of who I am and who I've been
I know that grace by definition
Is something I can never earn
But for all the things
That I may have missed
There's a lesson I believe
That I have learned

**CHORUS***
**There's a hand of kindness**
**Holding me, Holding me**
**There's a hand of kindness**
**Holding me, Holding on to me**

Forgiveness comes in
just  a moment
Sometimes the conse-
quences last
And it's hard to walk
inside that mercy
When the present is so
tied up to the past
In this crucible of cause
and effect
I walk the wire without
a net
And I wonder if I'll ever
fall too far
But that day has not
happened yet

**REPEAT CHORUS**
**And in the raven night, there shines a distant light**
**It seems to point at me, It burns away the night**
**Familiar figure on horizon, Moving closer now I see**
**His heart is shining like the sun**
**And He's reaching out to me**
**With a hand of kindness, He's holding me**

*Lifted up from the deep*

**This song was a precursor to other blessings we were yet to experience.**


Several months after Jason's death, Dave heard that Bob Bennett was coming to Kansas City. We immediately made arrangements to go to his concert. His song had touched our lives so profoundly that we felt it would be a gratifying privilege to meet him. I called the church and asked for details of the upcoming concert. I found myself sharing our story with the secretary of the church. She seemed moved and promised that Mr. Bennett would be told of how his song had impacted our lives.

That night, as we listened to the beautiful songs of this special musician, we felt a great sense of peace. As the concert was about to end, he told the crowd that he was going to sing one more song. He asked everyone to sing the chorus along with him.

I closed my eyes and squeezed Dave's hand as he began to sing *"Hand of Kindness."* Tears flowed from our eyes as everyone in the room joined in the chorus. Soon, everyone was singing a cappella. The voices sounded like a choir of prayers being lifted up to God. I wondered if Jason could hear the praises to God being sung in his memory.

We later met Bob Bennett and thanked him for using his gift to touch lives.

Even to this day, every time I hear this song, I imagine Jason going through the valley of death and looking straight ahead to see a shining "distant light" that burns away all the darkness. I imagine him with that big, beautiful smile on his face as he excitedly bellows, "**Awesome!**" In my mind's eye, I picture that beautiful light coming from the very heart of Jesus as He reaches out with His "hand of kindness" to welcome our son home. It is, as Jason would say, an *awesome* thought to envision Christ's "hand of kindness" holding our beloved son.

I wanted to capture our personal understanding of this song through a simple drawing that could be placed on Jay's headstone. Dave and I worked together to render that drawing.

The headstone is etched with two hands cupping a heart that bears Jay's name. Next to the engraving are the words from Bob Bennett's song, *"There's a hand of kindness holding me."*


*God's Song*

When we visit the grave, we always recall the song that God shared with us and we remember that our son is safely in God's hands.

We also used this same portrayal for the memorial award that was established in Jason's name...but I'll save that story for another chapter!

*"There's a hand of kindness holding me"*

# Chapter 7

# On Eagles' Wings

Through the course of 24 hours, our lives had changed completely. From the moment we received the phone call that drove me to my knees in empty prayer, to the time we found ourselves sitting in a funeral home making those "dreaded arrangements," God had confirmed His magnificent mercy in ways we could have never imagined:

> •*A beautiful song of hope before the twilight of our storm...*
> •*A glorious sign in the sky during the eerie stillness*
> *of our darkest hour...*
> •*A pure white dove to comfort our fears in the steely,*
> *cold hours of that morning after...*

I have an inscription hanging on a wall in our home that simply reads "Don't fear tomorrow. God is already there." **So true!** Before I even knew what to pray, God was already answering prayer.

Oh, how the answers to unspoken prayer were needed! The overpowering emotions we felt from losing our child were indescribably humbling.

It was as if I had become like a child myself...frightened, defenseless, needy. Just like a young girl who needs her father's reassurance that he still loves her and that "everything will be okay," I found myself clinging to my Heavenly Father tighter than ever before in my life. A daunting childlike weakness also prevailed at times. It was during those periods of frailty, in particular, that I ached for God's strength the most. I felt like one of those children in the song, *Jesus Loves Me* - "They are weak, but He is strong!"

After becoming so painfully humbled like a child, it was easy to receive God's gifts with pure, uncompromising faith and appreciation. It became almost natural to become totally dependent on God's love and strength alone. Maybe that's one example of the biblical teaching to "receive the kingdom of God as a little child." (If we could only learn to become like this in our everyday lives!)

We watched as that amazing source of strength filled Jenny just one day after her brother's death. On the very afternoon after Jay's accident, Jenny received a birthday card through the mail. It was from Jason and Wes. I nervously watched her as she read the card. Somehow through her tears, I could see a glimmer of resolve in her eyes.

Jason had always called his sister *Jen the Pen* or *Jenny Penny*. He had written: "Pen...hey girlfriend!...Happy Birthday!...Kick butt in track!...I will probably get to see you Friday...I might even beat this card home..."

The next day was Jenny's 17th birthday. It was also the "Mineral Water Classic" - an annual track meet for which she was scheduled to pole vault and run the 400-meter race. Jenny looked up from her card and tearfully, but assuredly, announced that she wanted to participate in the meet the next day.

Initially, I found myself discouraging Jenny from such a decision. She was so worn with grief. I was concerned she could injure herself by participating under such emotional duress and physical fatigue. Besides, what would people think? Would our grief look "wrong" if we were cheering at a track meet so soon after Jay's death? Would we appear disrespectful to some "expected standard" of the grieving process that we were now living?

(I have since realized that there is no *right* way or *wrong* way to grieve. There are no *distinct stages* of grief as I had been taught in my college psychology classes. Every loss is privately unique. Every mourner feels his own personal, undefined sorrow. That uniqueness should be honored with patience. It cannot be easily defined or methodically categorized.)

Jenny's desire to participate in the track meet had become deep-seeded and it would prove to be that hard, first step in the personal healing process for her. It became paramount that we honor and fully support her decision. To do otherwise would further wound our already heartbroken daughter.

Thank goodness Dave's family was with us. They have always been our kid's most avid supporters, going to countless numbers of events to cheer on our children. This track meet was probably the most important meet of Jenny's life. It was undoubtedly the hardest track meet for us to have ever attended. Having all the Simmons there with us was such a comfort as we made our first trip "out in public" since the accident.

It became obvious as we arrived at the stadium that this meet, and Jenny's performance in particular, were being dedicated to Jason. All of Jenny's teammates were wearing the number **19** - Jason's high school number.

My heart knew that Jenny was going to "give-it-her-all" one last time for her brother (one of her biggest fans)! Jay had planned to be here for his sister and (who knows) maybe God would allow him to "watch" his sister's dedication.

> *"but they that wait upon the lord shall renew their strength;*
> *They shall mount up with wings as eagles; they shall run,*
> *and not be weary;*
> *And they shall walk, and not faint."*
> Isaiah 40:31

As Jenny pole vaulted, I marveled at the strength she was given to clear the bar. Time and time again she "mounted up with wings as eagles" until she had vaulted herself above the bar to set a new school record.

Later, the Simmons family placed themselves strategically around the track to encourage Jenny through the grueling 400 meter race. As I watched her round the last curve and head toward the tape, she was easily 100 meters ahead of the rest of the runners. It seemed as though the entire stadium of fans was cheering her on. As she crossed the finish line, I instinctively ran to her, overwhelmed with emotion.

It didn't matter how high she had vaulted or how fast she had run the race. Two more gold medals didn't matter. She had plenty of medals. The important thing was that she caused others around her to question from where such strength and determination had come! It had come from her faith in God...a merciful God who had wished to honor her dedication to His newly received child.......our Jason!

Later that night after returning home from the track meet, Wes came into our room and laid in bed with us to share some precious thoughts.

Wes told us that as soon as he had received the phone call about Jay's accident, he fell on his knees and prayed. He told us his prayers were answered three times that night. First, he prayed that God would help him to drive to Kansas City safely. He then prayed that Jason could stay alive until he got there. Thirdly, he prayed that somehow Jason might know that he was there with him.

Wes made it to the hospital safely by about 2:30 that morning. Jay was still alive and when Wes took his brother's hand and talked to him, Jason's blood pressure and pulse rose significantly. Wes attributes this to answered prayer and to the character he believed his older brother to have.

Wes said that Jay was known for his big heart and for always giving everything 110% effort. As Wes put it, that big heart of Jay's kept on beating and with God's compassion, Jason was able to give that extra 110% effort one more time.

It had truly been an incredible day. It was so comforting for Dave and me to see God working immediately in our children's lives to strengthen and soothe them spiritually.

Jay would have been so proud - proud of his tender-hearted "Jenny Penny" who loved him enough to perform in a physically grueling event...proud of that "physically tough linebacker" who could reach down into the depths of his tender heart to express beautiful words of remembrance for his big brother.

Oh, if Jay could tell them anything, I know he would let them know that he is still their biggest fan - rooting them on toward the true victory in this life!

Jay now knows with certainty the truth about death. Death can be "tackled!" That was accomplished by his Savior at Calvary. Jay also learned as he crossed the "finish line of this race we call life" that he could raise his hand in victory!

> *"this is the victory that overcometh the world...*
> *Our faith."*
>
> 1 John 5:4b

*Lifted up from the deep*

# Chapter 8

# God's Rainbow

Looking back, I found the day of the visitation harder to face than the day of the funeral. The morning before visitation was the first time we would confront the reality that our young, vivacious son now lay - stilled and silenced - in a coffin.

It is not my intent to be morose in my remembrance of this experience, but this cold, curt statement accurately describes the agonizing and abrupt reality of our loss.

As Dave has so often expressed, our physical bodies are only "the boxes we come in." I know and believe that after death we receive beautiful new spiritual bodies beyond our comprehension. In the depths of such tender grief, however, it was hard to embrace God's promise.

All I could think was that this boy we loved and cherished had been "wrapped" in a physical body that we had held and hugged and nurtured....

> It was the "bottom" we had spanked...
> The belly we had tickled...
> The back we had patted...

I adored his glistening smile and his deep, caring eyes. I ached to hold him once again. Even though he was a 22 year old man, I could only think of him now as "my baby boy." I wanted to *kiss him and make it all better!* That's what I did when he was young, but this beautiful body had been broken beyond a mother's kiss. That bitter reality consumed me as we walked into the funeral home on that gloomy morning.

Our son was **really** gone and this passage into the funeral home would force us to face that sobering truth squarely in the face. I recognized the fact that I would literally and painfully grieve the loss of every part of him - including his physical body...a reality I had not yet allowed myself to face.

A flood of pain filled my heart!

*God's Rainbow*

"What Noah Saw"

Today, Lord, I so desperately need
For you to give *me* all that you gave Noah...
Faith, to follow a course I cannot comprehend.
Wisdom, to build a worthy ark.
Peace, when the rains fall and the floodwaters rise...
And finally, your precious promise!

O Lord, I so need to see
What Noah saw...
I'm so ready for
My rainbow!

By Joy Morgan Davis
From the book, I'm Ready for My Rainbow, Lord

After the initial stinging jolt of going into the funeral home that morning, a surprising peace overcame me. Although the "emotional storm" was clearly still surrounding us, my heart had been calmed and the "clouds of despair" had been lifted enough to allow me to see my way through the rest of this difficult day.

As the time for the actual visitation approached, Dave expressed concern about the weekend forecast. Remembering his drive home on the day of Jay's accident, Dave recalled his preoccupation with gardening plans before the predicted deluge of heavy rain. We were expecting so many friends and family from out-of-town. There was an overflow crowd anticipated for our small church. Pastor Dave had even talked of setting up speakers for listening to the service from outside the church if that became necessary. Dave had been earnestly praying that the rain chances might diminish from the forecast.

When Dave mentioned this appeal to God, I recalled the morning after Jason died. He had held me in his arms and promised that we would unceasingly pray our way through every detail of this journey. One of the first things we prayed during those first few days was to receive a peaceful night's sleep. After we had asked...we received...and we slept

*Lifted up from the deep*

through the night.

On the surface, praying for *no rain* seemed like a simple, inconsequential prayer. How many times had we frivolously prayed "Please don't let it rain" when we felt that rain might be an inconvenience to our personal lives? Dave, however, was genuinely concerned about the possibility of heavy rain. To seriously and faithfully ask the very **Maker of the Rain** to personally monitor it for *our sake* was a major request!

As we approached the funeral home, a bolt of lightning flashed and rumbled across the clouds. The sky opened and rain gushed out in torrents upon us. We ran into the funeral home and presumed that God's answer to Dave's prayer was an obviously loud and thunderous "No!"

Our concern about the rain temporarily passed as we worked our way through the crowd of people who were there to share our grief. It was truly an overwhelming encounter with the beautiful *gift of friendship* which God allows us to experience in this life.

The time we shared with others that night was a true blessing and is a precious treasure to us now:

It was an evening devoted entirely to sharing reflections
and fond memories of Jason.

It was a cherished time of learning things about our son
that we had not known before.

It was an endearing chance to hear about ways Jason had
touched other's lives.

For those precious few hours we were surrounded by people who helped to fill our emptiness with their love for Jason. We were being emotionally and spiritually lifted above the floodwaters of our grief by people who sought to share our sadness.

There were as many different emotions expressed that evening as there were different personalities passing through to speak with us. This warm gathering of friends and family collectively represented the many stages of our lives. Sharing memories with so many provided us a priceless opportunity to reflect upon Jason's life from many different perspectives. It allowed us to enjoy a panoramic remembrance of his life, from the time of his birth through the time of his "recent past" as a college senior.

Some people expressed an anger about the accident...an anger we had not allowed ourselves to feel. Others shared a heartfelt, but tender joy that Jason would no longer suffer the injustices of this cold world.

A few questioned the reasons why this had happened to Jason rather than to some "thug" out on the streets. Several reverently "rejoiced" that it was Jason who was called, rather than someone who did not yet know his Savior

Some were trembling.Some were sobbing. Some were nervously chattering. Many were speechless. At times, it felt as though we were comforting our friends as much as they were comforting us.

Every shared memory, every expression of sorrow, every shed tear, every warm hug helped to calm our "storm." We felt endeared to each individual there. Everyone gave of themselves as best they knew how. Each reached out to us, shared our grief and helped us to confront our sorrow.

*Lifted up from the deep*

God tells us to share each other's problems.
*"Bear ye one another's burdens,*
*And so fulfill the law of Christ."*
Galatians 6:2

I had never considered any deep, hidden meaning behind this passage of scripture. Helping each other out in times of need simply seems like the "right thing to do." A friend of ours who had been with us at the hospital later shared her thoughts about "bearing each other's burdens." I found Mary Ellen's thoughts to be simple, yet profound:

*"I am surprised to find that I am still grieving with you daily. It's difficult (perhaps impossible) to explain. It is not simply 'being sad because I have friends who are hurting.' It's so much more than that. <u>It's a spiritual and mysterious sharing of grief.</u> For a couple of weeks after Jason's death, I would awaken early and immediately all of you and Jason would fill my mind and heart. I started each morning in quiet reflection and prayer for all of you. I no longer wake early, but you are still first in my thoughts when I do, and remain a constant presence throughout each day. I realize that what I am experiencing must be like a tiny kernel of the tremendous grief you bear. It may be a mistake to try to explain this, but somehow it's an experience in the true brotherhood of Christ, and a blessing to be allowed to share your sorrow. <u>**Wouldn't it be something if that is how God enables us to bear our sorrows-by literally passing small grains of our burden to others in his family?!**</u>"*

I know without question that every person who was willing to receive even a small portion of our sorrow was strengthening us immeasurably. The truth is that we are all vulnerable to feelings of weakness as we confront the certainty of death. That's why we *all* need each other. I could see that truth in the tears of these wonderful people. I could hear it in their words of comfort. I could feel it in their hugs.

Suddenly in the midst of this room full of sadness, I looked up and saw the smiling face of my dear friend, Cindi. What a welcomed sight. I hadn't seen a smile in what now seemed "an eternity."

Cindi and her husband, Gary, had gone to the airport to pick up Aaron, my brother's oldest son. I hadn't seen him since Chris' funeral. Cindi was glowing with excitement as she told me "The rainbow is back!" She knew the importance of the rainbow to my family. I had told her all about the rainbows that had comforted us when Chris died. She wanted me to know that there was "the most beautiful rainbow she had ever seen." They first saw it at the airport as Aaron got off the plane.

As I tightly hugged my brother's son, I wondered if maybe this rainbow was purposely for him...a young man who was still grieving the recent loss of his dad. Because of the large crowd, I was unable to get outside to see God's gift to *anyone* who would choose to embrace it.

As the visitation came to a close, I felt exhausted. I wanted to leave this scene, but I was also reluctant to walk out those doors. The next time we would be near our son's body would be at the funeral itself. I could feel the "flood of pain" starting to surface again.

As our family left the funeral home, I glanced back over my shoulder. Through tear-filled eyes, we all looked toward the heavens. God slowly decorated the sky with another glorious rainbow.

This was **our rainbow**...or so it felt!

*"O Lord, I so need to see what Noah saw.*
*I'm so ready for my rainbow!"*
(By Joy Morgan Davis)

The rain that fell as we entered the funeral home that evening was the only rain that fell through the rest of the weekend. God answered Dave's prayer in such a glorious way. He gave us just enough rain to create a much needed rainbow. He also abated the rain for our son's funeral.

*Lifted up from the deep*

The waves of grief continued to ebb and flow through our hearts. As we journeyed through these "uncharted waters" of sorrow, we were continually lifted up by God's "ark of protection and comfort." Just as it was in Noah's day, God was faithful to remind us that the raging waters of the storm would eventually subside.

His precious promise of hope was splendidly displayed in the sign of his rainbow. Just as the dove had left Noah's ark when the waters abated, the dove that had nested here during our initial deluge of sorrow would soon leave our presence and never return.

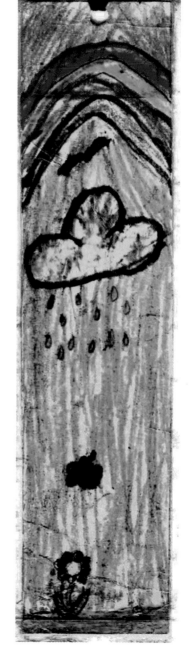

*"and God remembered Noah..."*
*(*Genesis 8:1)

**We, too, felt remembered in the midst of our storm!**

(Copy of a bookmark made by Jason, 3rd grade, 1985)

*God's Rainbow*

# Chapter 9

# The Goodbye

### April 26, 1998

It was hard to believe, but only two weeks earlier we had all been rushing around preparing for Easter Sunday services. What a wonderful day that had been! The exhilaration of lively interaction between the kids was now only a fond memory. That memory haunted me as we once again readied ourselves for church. Our preparation for this particular service, however, was painstakingly slow and methodical.

On Easter Sunday, April 12, 1998, we had gone into a "house of celebration." On April 26, 1998, we were entering into a "house of mourning." I felt profound anguish as I prepared to attend a funeral service that, in essence, would represent a final goodbye.

God had faithfully been by our side and had blessed us immensely through these early days of our trial. He had given us incredible *gifts of comfort.* We had been allowed to witness the strength of our children's spiritual growth as they put *their* trust in God. I knew we could count on Him to stay by our side on this day, too. That was my prayer as we entered the church.

> *"In the midst of the church*
> *will I sing praise unto thee.*
> *And again, I will put my trust in Him.*
> *And again, behold I and the children which God hath given me."*
> Hebrews 2:12-13

God had given us three precious children. We cherished the support and grace He had given to Jenny and Wes. I wondered what kinds of *gifts of comfort* God had given to our dying child as he entered the valley.

I ached to share some parting gift of love with Jay. My only gift to him now would have to be in the form of prayer. My heart's prayer was that Jay had put all his trust in God and had profoundly felt the overpowering strength of God's love as Jesus defended our precious son against death.

I wondered what Jason saw as the gates of heaven opened:

### *The Goodbye*

*"For every one that asketh receiveth; and he that seeketh findeth;*
*and to him that knocketh it shall be opened ;*
*Or what man is there of you, whom if his son ask bread,*
*Will he give him a stone?*
*Or if he ask a fish, will he give him a serpent?*
*If ye then, being evil, know how to give good gifts unto your*
*children,*
*How much more shall your Father which is in heaven*
*Give good things to them that ask him?"*

Matthew 7: 8-11

My greatest source of comfort was to trust that God loves our son more than we are capable of loving him. I know how immeasurable our love is for our children. I honestly cannot grasp the enormity and depth of God's love for **His** children!

Through that infinite love, God had surely given Jason "good gifts" beyond our comprehension. Most assuredly, God had given him the ultimate gift of all...**the gift of eternal life!**

Just two weeks earlier, when we had celebrated that glorious gift during the Easter service, tears of pride had filled my eyes as Jay approached the altar to read that poem. My eyes were now filled with tears of grief as my son's body lay in front of that very same altar poetry being recited in his memory. Through my unrelenting sadness, however, emerged that ever-present pride for my son. He was truly a charitable young man who had touched many lives.

I was very aware that the sanctuary was filled with people from all walks of life. I prayed that this service and our circumstances would change at least one person's life forever. I wanted the memory of Jason's charitable life, as well as the reality of his sudden death, to honor God by leading someone to think about Christ. That would be a glorious legacy. If I could see that happen to **just one person**, maybe I could some day embrace this painful juncture that God had planned for our lives.

❖❖❖❖❖❖❖❖❖❖

*Lifted up from the deep*

<u>Pastor Dave spoke God's truth simply, but eloquently</u>:
(excerpts from pastor Dave's funeral notes)

"I would like to leave you with three things to ponder in your hearts today:

1) There was a great German theologian named Karl Barth - a great student of the Bible for many years. While once traveling in America, he was asked a profound question...'What is the single greatest theological truth you've discovered?' To which he simply replied, 'Jesus loves me, this I know...for the Bible tells me so.'

"Yes, Jesus loves you. He loves you with an everlasting love; and underneath you are His everlasting arms (John 31:3 and Deuteronomy 33:27). You are on a roller coaster ride of emotions. I was struck with how God has given this family gifts of grace to sustain you. Saturday evening after the visitation at the funeral home, there was a beautiful rainbow arching across the sky. Also, the day after the accident Grandma Virginia noticed a white dove nesting on her back porch, which is still there. The dove is a beautiful symbol of peace, joy, love and especially of the Holy Spirit. Yes, as John 3:16 says, 'God so loved the world that he gave his only begotten Son, that whosoever believeth in Him should not perish, but have everlasting life.'

2) If you were born...you <u>will</u> also die! It is a fact of life! Jason could have told me that...I could have told Jason that. The only questions are when and how. I don't know! Only God knows that. 'It's appointed unto man once to die, then the judgment.'
<u>Judgment</u>...that's when we find out where we'll spend eternity. Beyond death is eternity. The scriptures say there are two places in eternity...heaven and hell.

3) God has made a way for us to spend eternity in heaven. We live in a world where it's politically correct

<u>The Goodbye</u>

to believe in many ways...to your own spiritual fulfillment, your own revelation of God, your own way to
heaven. 'There is a way that seemeth right unto man, but
the end of it is the ways of death.' (Proverbs 14:12).
There is only one way to heaven (John 14:6). This is how
you can be saved...Romans 10:9.

"Our grieving is different than the world's grieving. We Christians
grieve with hope. I Peter 1:3-5 tells us that we have been born into a
living hope and the inheritance that is in heaven.
"Wes, you were right when you didn't say goodbye to Jason...you just
said 'We'll see each other again.'
"Jenny, yes, we are all a little bit jealous of Jason...he's there in
heaven now and knows what it's like to be with the Lord!"

Ever since October 8, 1975, God had entrusted us with Jason's life.
On April 23, 1998, we needed to trust God with our son's physical death.
For those 22 wonderful years we had been given the privilege of
loving, nurturing, and training this precious gift from God. Now, God
alone held Jason's life for all eternity.
The regrets about mistakes we made as the parents of this boy were
overwhelming. There could be no question that we loved Jason as much
as any parent could love his child. Throughout the course of those 22
years, however, I knew that we had disappointed God on more than one
occasion. I asked God's forgiveness for those mistakes. I knew there
would be no more mistakes now that Jay was totally in God's care.

> *"I will ransom them from the power of the grave...*
> *I will redeem them from death."*
>
> Hosea 13:14

Dave calls the grave our "launching pad." Those simple words
beautifully describe God's profound promise!

*Lifted up from the deep*

**It was on this promise that I hung all my hope
as I left my son's grave.**

Returning home that afternoon, we came upon a highway accident. It became obvious as we passed the scene that another family of lives had been abruptly turned upside-down by the sudden, unexpected death of a loved one.

Another family was about to embark upon this grievous journey...
another family who, like us just days ago, thought that
"this day would be like any other day."

We later discovered that a young, 18-year-old girl
had died in the accident.

May God help us all...for we are all a needy people...
In all places and at all times!

# Chapter 10

# The Belt

### *You Have Been Good*

*If I never get to see another rainbow*
*Or share another laugh with a friend*
*If I never stand barefoot by the ocean*
*Or get to kiss my child goodnight again*

*You have been good*
*You have been good*
*And I am in wonder*
*How could it be*
*You have been good*
*You've been so good*
*In so many ways*
*You've been good to me*

(Words and music by

Scott Krippayne & Tony Wood)

God had been so good to us throughout those early days of our "new life."

That is exactly what this *life-changing* trial seemed to become ...our "new life." It felt as though time had stopped on April 23, 1998. "Life as we knew it" became a thing of the past. I found myself relating to time in terms of "since Jason died..."

...*Since Jason died*, we had been given more gracious gifts from God than we could have ever expected or deserved. I knew that God was the only one we could fully depend on to get through our grief. I knew that we needed to put Him in total control of our lives.....we were broken and I counted on God to "fix" us.

I recognized beyond question that without God's compassionate comfort and constant encouragement, we would never recover from our loss of Jason.

### *The Belt*

All the people had gone home

The dove had flown away.

The song still lingered in our hearts.

The rainbow was gone...for now.

The 50-year sign in the sky was a vivid remembrance,
but only Jason had
"gone home to his original owner."

We were still here with gaping holes in our hearts.

Several days had passed and Dave left to go to Maryville where Jason had attended college. He had gone to gather Jason's "earthly possessions." It was the first time I had been alone since the accident. It was also the first time I couldn't hide behind countless distractions.

As hard as I tried to avoid the haunting pain of my most intimate thoughts, my mind kept racing toward the same set of questions - Was Jason **really** saved? Did he **really** love Jesus? Did he choose to become baptized for all the **right** reasons and not just to make his parents happy? Had he been given enough time to genuinely love the Lord? I wondered to what "degree" one needed to love the Lord in order to be saved.

Did all these doubts represent a questioning of **Jason's** faith
Or a test of my own faith?
My mind was reeling!

I had witnessed firsthand the emerging faith of Wes and Jenny as they were forced to confront their brother's death. They could have turned their backs on God out of anger. Instead, they seemed to firmly grasp hold of God's love. Their actions and words encouraged me immensely and I could perceive that they were on a course of spiritual growth.

I had no tangible confirmation of the growth of Jason's faith. I had never seen his faith "put to the test." I thought about my urgent prayers

*Lifted up from the deep*

to God after my brother's death - *that he draw all my family closer to him.*

Certainly, the members of our family were presently being drawn closer to God as we begged for His mercy to save us from our grief; but what about Jason? Had Jay, himself, been drawn closer to God? Had God already answered this prayer prior to Jay's death? How could I possibly know for sure now that Jason was gone?

❖❖❖❖❖❖❖❖❖❖

Dave returned from Maryville later that same afternoon. Seeing and touching Jay's possessions was so bitter sweet. The smell of cologne hung on his clothes. As I savored the aroma, I fleetingly felt as though he was still here. Flipping through his photographs made my heart rejoice as I remembered happy times in his brief life.

Somehow as I scanned over the few boxes that Dave brought home, I felt a "silly sorrow" that Jason actually had so few possessions. I was shocked at myself for feeling sad about something like that! I found myself sobbing as I picked up a set of plastic containers that he had used to organize his leftovers. These "things" were so inconsequential, but they tore at my heart in an unexpected anguish.

I suppose the viewing of his possessions - or lack of them - reminded me of the simple, unassuming nature of Jay's life. That simplicity was the hallmark of his charm and it was especially endearing to me.

My eyes then focused on his weight-lifting belt. The confirmation of answered prayer once again filled my heart. Across the belt in Jay's handwriting were the words, **Jesus, My Savior**.

This discovery was profoundly stirring. To find these words written on the leather of his belt seemed providential. I could feel that much needed assurance from God. He gave us this *gift of discovery* to understand that indeed Jason knew and appreciated from where all his true strength must come - not in what we can do to empower ourselves, but by the might that Christ gives us to overcome this world.

> **Jason understood the bottom line**...
> *and it is that bottom line that saved his soul*...
> that he was a sinner, that he needed a savior,
> and that his savior is Jesus

*The Belt*

Thank you, God, for spoken prayers answered!

---

### You Have Been Good
*(continued)*

*If I never have another prayer that's answered*
*Or have another blessing come my way*
*If this is all I know of heaven's kindness*
*Father, I would still have to say*

*You have been good*
*You have been good*
*And I am in wonder*
*How could it be*
*You have been good*
*You've been so good*
*In so many ways*
*You've been good to me*

(Words and music by
Scott Krippayne and Tony Wood)

---

As we continued to search through Jason's things, I felt an awkward uneasiness. Although I relished every memory of him that I could glean by exploring his belongings, I didn't want to *violate his privacy.*

What an incredibly peculiar concern that seemed to be! Maybe a more candid fear was that I might find something that would bruise my sterling memory of him. I know that deep down inside my "mothering heart" was the troubling possibility that I might discover something that would reveal hurtful times in his life. I couldn't bear to think about those times, but I knew they had existed. I was sure that I had even been the cause of some of those hurts! I recalled the last time we had talked with Jay. No matter what our reasons were as parents, I was sure he was disappointed and possibly even *hurt* to hear "no" about buying that

*Lifted up from the deep*

acreage he had called about.

Suddenly something downstairs interrupted the stillness of our solemn reflection! No one else was in the house and it sounded as though something had fallen. We hurried down the stairs. I was shocked to find a picture laying on the living room floor. It was the portrait of Jason that my dad had painted when Jason was just a baby. My heart sunk and an eerie despair overcame me.

Dave quickly picked up the portrait, re-worked the frame and hung the cherished picture back in its special place on the wall.

I immediately became strangely protective about the incident - much like a parent defending the honor of her child. Anger quickly stirred in my heart - much like a parent enraged at any injustices facing her child. *I then became apprehensive.* **What had caused the picture to fall off the wall?**

I wanted to call this disturbing occurrence *a fluke.* I wanted to simply explain it away.....the hanger or nail that held the picture had just suddenly "let go." It was a simple result of "cause and effect."

No matter how hard I tried to avoid them, however, my thoughts were pursuing another very distinct possibility. I was nagged by a prospect that I did not want to consider...

...We never once considered the song, the conjunction of the moon, the dove, or the rainbows to be mere coincidences. We considered them all to be timely gifts from God because we know that God is real.

Why should a fallen picture of our fallen child create such havoc with the peace that God had given us - "*...the peace of God, which passeth all understanding,*" (Philippians 4:7).

There was only one explanation - Satan, too, is real! Just as God has a plan <u>for</u> us, Satan has a plan <u>against</u> us. He would immensely enjoy putting doubt and discouragement into our lives.

*"For we wrestle not against flesh and blood,*
*but against principalities,*
*against powers, against the rulers of the darkness of this world,*
*against spiritual wickedness in high places."*

Ephesians 6:12

We know that the battle has to be fought on our knees. The only way

Satan could take away our peace about Jason's eternal welfare was if we allowed him to do so.

*"Submit yourselves therefore to God.*
*Resist the devil,*
*And he will flee from you."*

James 4:7

I often pick up that weightlifting belt and think about our true source of strength. It's in the belief expressed by my son's simple inscription.

This is a depiction of the drawing on Jay's belt.
It is the same depiction that is etched on our son's headstone.

*Lifted up from the deep*

# Chapter 11

# A Year of Firsts

The first Mother's Day...the first Father's Day...the first family reunion...on and on it goes...

How would each of us as individuals and as a redefined family unit conform our lives to all these "firsts" - *since Jason died?* I felt a gnawing ache in the pit of my stomach with the approach of each special occasion circled on the calendar. A wave of "longing" would swallow up any joy I might manage to garner. I was homesick for our *yesterdays* as a "family of five." At times it felt like the "wind had been knocked out of me" as grief would literally "take my breath away" when I would speak of upcoming special events.

An awkward guilt consumed me as I searched for the missing joy I had always experienced in sharing these special times with my children and family. I was painfully aware that my sorrow over Jason's absence was overpowering my usual delight in creating new memories.

Fall was just around the corner and college football was about to begin. Going to watch Wes play football was always "an event" for us. Packing up the car and traveling to the games had become a routine that we cherished.

As Dave, Jenny and I waited in the stadium for the start of the first game of the 1998 season, that all-familiar gnawing in my gut resurfaced. One on Wes' biggest fans was no longer sitting in the stands.

The Bearcats ran out on the field and the crowd cheered their "hometown heroes" into a new season. I immediately searched for number "44." I found my linebacker right in the middle of the pack. As always, he looked big and strong and excited. One thing was different...on each arm was a band. One armband sported the number "19" (Jason's football number). On the other band were Jay's initials, **JDS.** I instantly thought about Wes' pledge the night Jason died...that the Northwest Missouri State Bearcats would win a National Championship for his brother!

This game was the beginning of that venture toward Wes' pledge, and it proved to be the first win in what would become an unprecedented, perfect 15 - 0 season for the Bearcats!

*A Year of Firsts*

**The Bearcats were, indeed, headed to Florence, Alabama, for the NCAA Division II National Championship Game!**

This team was unique...each player cared deeply for one another. In fact, many of the players and coaches had come to Jason's funeral in warm support for Wes and our family. I held a special place in my heart for these young men.

We felt especially privileged that Wes had been placed under the guidance of head coach Mel Tjeerdsma. He was a godly man who taught his team much more than the fundamentals of good football. After each game, Coach Tjeerdsma could be seen standing in the middle of his kneeling football players as a prayer was offered up to God.

The prayers weren't about winning ball games. The prayers were about honoring God. This act of praising God on every 50-yard line of every football stadium they played spoke volumes to Dave and me.

Midway through this very special season, Wes had made another precious dedication to his brother. It was early October when I told Wes to "do something special" at the upcoming game in commemoration of Jay's birthday. Although my request was really made in jest, I cried *tears of joy* as Wes made an interception and ran the ball into the end zone for the very first touchdown of his college career! TEARS OF JOY...what a wonderful emotion that was to experience in my life again!

Through the course of the season, several newspaper articles were written about Wes' dedication of the season to Jason. It was as though Jay had become the "twelfth man" on the team. My greatest delight was stirred when the papers quoted Wes' pronouncements of God's help in dealing with the death of his brother. Wes had been "given a stage" and he used that stage to acknowledge the importance of God in his life. That stage was about to become even larger as we headed to Alabama for a game that would be broadcast on national TV.

The game was televised on ESPN and Wes' story was tenderly reported throughout the broadcast. The Florence, Alabama, local paper also covered this "human-interest" story in very personal, touching detail. Coach Tjeerdsma was quoted as finding it "ironic that the Bearcats needed a tragedy to develop such a common bond."

He told reporters that he thought "Jason's death just showed how close this team really is."

Excerpts from *The Times Daily*, December 9, 1998
Todd Thompson/Sports Writer

We are all *players* on the team known as "The Brotherhood of Man." Likewise, it is ironic that we <u>all</u> have a *common bond* which develops from the result of a tragedy - the tragedy that occurred in the Garden of Eden. Each of us faces choices and adversities in our personal battle against that fierce opponent who wants to steal our eternal victory.

As "Coach" God builds His squad, He seems to deliberately place others on our team who can strengthen our bond with Him, as well as with one another. He can use shared heartbreak to help unify His "team" and to make us all "better players." **He definitely expects us to be "team players" by lifting each other up:**

*"Two are better than one;*
*because they have a good reward for their labour.*
*For if they fall, the one will lift up his fellow:*
*but woe to him that is alone when he falleth;*
*for he hath not another to help him up."*
*"And if one prevail against him, two shall*
*withstand him;*
*and a threefold cord is not quickly broken."*

Ecclesiastes 4:9-10 &12

If we are willing to listen to our "Coach" and learn to "play the game" as He taught us, we will become victorious when we find ourselves at the "last play of the game."

With the defensive help of our "teammates" and with a strong offense of unyielding faith in our "Coach," not only will we win the game.......

WE WILL WIN THE ETERNAL CHAMPIONSHIP!

*A Year of Firsts*

The Bearcat football season became another example of how God answers prayer in so many different ways. The strategies in His "playbook" are as infinite as the universe He created. His grace is more abundant than I could have ever imagined.

Our family had come to the realization that this particular football season was another beautiful gift from God.

•It had become the "vessel covered in pigskin" that God used
to introduce joy back into our lives.
•It had become the "medicine wrapped in newsprint" that
God used to show us the healing effect of
sharing our grief with others.
•It had become the "touchdown of mercy" that God used
to assure us that He loves us personally and
knows our deepest hopes...

**The greatest personal joy we derived from this season was the assurance once again from God that He truly loves our children!**

Just as He had honored Jenny's dedication to Jay at the track meet, He also granted Wes a championship tribute to Jason's memory...

The 1998 football season became known by Bearcat fans as
"A Season to Remember."

Rightfully so. The Bearcats became the National Champions!

This was the first time in the history of Northwest Missouri State University that any athletic team had won a national championship.

• It took a lot of talent and determination and heart!
• It took a bit of luck!
• It took an awesome God who can use even the gruffest game of
football to honor the heartfelt wish of a grief-stricken linebacker,
while reaching out to the tender hearts of many in the
"Brotherhood of Man."

*Lifted up from the deep*

With the end of a prolonged football season, Christmas was at hand. I knew that this holiday would be extremely hard to face. Confronting the countless number of memories and family traditions that encompass this particular time of year seemed insurmountable.

Not only was this our first Christmas without Jason, it was also the first since my brother had died. To ignore the absence of Jason and Chris was impossible. To bypass the holiday all together was a ridiculous notion. To leave town would not make the pain go away. We had no choice but to gather together as a family and experience the reality of the first of all future Christmas holidays *without* our loved ones.

Just days before Christmas, I was deeply touched to receive a gift from a long-time college friend of mine. Marie had kept in very close contact with me since Jay's accident and she had lovingly sent us an ornament for our tree. It was a beautiful, hand-painted egg. The artist had painted a deer on the egg. Little did Marie realize the significance of that painting to us.

I instantly thought of Jason when I saw the ornament. Jason was an avid deer hunter and I immediately cherished this gift as a precious reminder of him. As I hung the ornament on our tree, I felt blessed to have discovered a new tradition for my Christmas holidays. I would find and place a specially selected ornament on our tree each year in memory of Jason. It was a small drop of comfort in the vast void I needed to fill, but I felt unexplained comfort in finding some tangible way of keeping Jason a part of our future Christmas experiences.

On Christmas Eve, Jenny and Wes were especially excited that Dave and I open their gifts to us. It was obvious that they had put a lot of thought and love into these gifts. I took a deep breath as I opened the first package.

Wes had brought an especially priceless gift to us from the university. It was Jason's college diploma. Even though Jay's life was cut short before completing the requirement for this diploma, the college wanted to award him the Bachelor's Degree in Mathematics that he had worked so hard to achieve. I sobbed. It was at that point that we all cried and held each other as we openly and honestly mourned Jay's absence from this beloved family evening.

As Dave and I opened the next present, we were delighted to receive a precious gift of love from Wes. He had sculpted a box that artistically expressed different aspects of Jay's life and death. On the lid, he had molded hands holding a heart, as is etched on Jay's headstone. Wes, however, had added a priceless detail to his portrayal of the "Hands of Kindness" - a detail that I am sorry we overlooked when we designed the headstone. Wes had placed a nail hole in each hand - the most important detail of God's love for us and the place where we rest all of our hope!

Jenny then presented us with a piece of her heart. Inside her gift was a book she had crafted, filled with special family photographs and stories and poetry which she had authored. Throughout the entire book she had intertwined the beautiful imagery of the rainbow. *"A rainbow is the ribbon on God's gift of hope."* (Author Unknown). Her gift was a beautiful illustration of our family's shared hope and of her love for her family.

Both Jenny and Wes had creatively expressed their individual and sincere appreciation for God's wonderful graces through these difficult months. Not only did their gifts bless us deeply, they were also priceless tributes to Jay's memory. They honored God's compassion for our family and they beautifully acknowledged the loss we were each feeling.

Another new family tradition emerged later that Christmas eve. Dave gathered us around the dining room table. We held hands and Dave led us in prayer. He then shared several scriptures:

He read first from 2 Corinthians 5:8 - *"We are confident, I say, and willing rather to be absent from the body, and to be present with the Lord."*

He then recited from Matthew 18:20, when Christ told his disciples, *"For where two or three are gathered together in my name, there am I in the midst of them."*

With tears flowing from his eyes, Dave then offered me and our precious children his heartfelt thoughts. He explained that since we know that God has promised to be in our midst when we gather in His name, and since Jason is now present with the Lord, we can still remain joined together as a "family of five" through the connection of our worship of Christ. At that point we each shared Communion for the first time in our home. For me, this moment was of such sacred proportions that I could not contain the emotion and passion I was experiencing.

I knew that each future Christmas would bring new cherished memories for our family. I knew that we would always include Jason in our celebrations. I've come to an indisputable understanding that as long as we continue to gather together as God's children, we will remain *"a family of five."*

For reasons I never really understood, we lost contact with Jason's fiancée Melissa. She was such a vital link to a special part of Jason's life. I had promised my son as he lay dying in the hospital that I would do all I could to help Melissa through her loss. I don't know if he could hear me...I'm not sure I even verbalized the promise...but I knew that if he could ask anything of me it would be to take care of Melissa. I never got that opportunity.

As strange as it may seem, I had looked forward to nurturing and caring for Melissa on behalf of my son. I ached to grieve with her - getting details of his last day on this earth and sharing memories of the young man that we both loved.

We eventually discovered through an announcement in the paper that Mel had married a man from her home town. Friends in the community later told us that she was expecting a baby sometime in early spring.

I felt very mixed emotions about the news. I was glad that she was "getting on with her life" and I prayed that she would have a happy future with her new found family. At the same time, I prayed forgiveness for the resentment and hurt I was feeling that someone else was living out Jason's dreams of a future with the girl he had chosen to marry.

The first Easter was a bittersweet reminder of the wonderful Easter we had shared the year before. My memories of that wonderful "last time together" kept me afloat in the flood of melancholy pangs I felt to see my son again. I wished so desperately that I might see Jason's face or hear his voice, even if only in a dream. I had experienced several wonderful dreams throughout the first few months after Jay died. Those dreams were so comforting and I always considered them to be blessings from God.

I awoke the morning after Easter and told Dave that I had, in fact, dreamt about Jay the night before. The images in my dream were so real that I actually felt as though I had experienced Jason's powerful voice, his beautiful smile, his deep caring eyes.

As I awoke that morning, I pondered the paradox of feelings that dreams invoke. My dream made me feel as though I had spent precious time with Jason again, but my awakening from these *images in the night* profoundly emphasized the fact that his actual presence in our lives was no longer a reality. Although the dream was a blessing, it also dramatically stirred the longing in my heart.

My dream conveyed to me that Melissa had given birth to her baby on March 18. In my sleep I could visualize Jason telling me that he was taking Melissa out for the evening to "give her a break from the stresses of having a baby." That caring, giving attitude was so typical of Jason's character. However, my dreamt reaction toward Jason's kindness was all too reflective of the deep, "real-life" resentment I knew I was feeling. Before I could express my disapproval of Jay's support, I suddenly woke up.

I was particularly mystified by the date in my dream. It was so pronounced in my mind that I made sure I verbalized the exact date to Dave and to my friend, Cindi. I was gripped with a passionate desire to find out if the baby had, in fact, been born on March 18.

A week or so later a friend at work handed me the local paper from Melissa's home town. As I flipped through the pages I came to the section of the paper that listed birth announcements. There it was! I could hardly believe my eyes! Melissa's baby **was**, in fact, born on March 18!

As I reflected on this chain of events, I wondered why I had experienced such a dream. Was it just a coincidence or one of those "weird things that happen" in this life? On the other hand, could the dream be from God? If the dream **was** from Him, what was I to glean from the experience? For days I pondered the meaning of the dream.

I thought about the many examples given in the Bible of how God uses dreams to encourage and instruct His people. The Bible indicates that God sometimes uses dreams to reveal His will to others. I felt that it was biblically-based to consider that God might use a dream to teach me something. After all, He had used everything from a song to a football game to heal our broken hearts.

I prayed for understanding.

A few days later I felt as though a caption had been written under the "picture of my dream" explaining the imagery I had experienced. I pray that my understanding of the dream is God-given and not self-driven.

> The kind and compassionate heart that Jason displayed in my dream would seem to represent the Christ-likeness that my son has now inherited from his new birth. After all, someone who has been reborn **in** Christ, would become **like** Christ. Although that should be our never-ending goal in this earthly realm, the evidence of that goal being realized would shine brightly as we are clothed in the gift of His righteousness in the spiritual realm.
>
> It dawned on me that I was not allowed to share any resentments with Jay in the dream. The *"are you crazy"* lecture that I was about to deliver to him was immediately cut short when I suddenly woke up. Was this a signal for me to let go of any offense or anger I felt about Melissa's situation since Jason died? Did my heart need to forgive her for "getting on with her life" in a way that I didn't understand and in a way that was really none of my business?
>
> I knew that my anger could not serve the cause of Christ.
>
> > *"For the wrath of man worketh not*
> > *the righteousness of God."*
> >
> > James 1:20
>
> My prayer became that all bitterness in my heart would subside and that I would become more "Christ-

like" myself as I dealt with this particular occurrence in my life - a situation that affected me emotionally, but was really only a shadow hiding in the perimeter of my personal life.

I later wrote to Mel and shared some of my thoughts about this dream with her. The fact that I had dreamed the actual date of her baby's birth seemed significant to me. I felt as though the date had a *signature from God* attached to it - the "handwriting on the wall" - telling me to pay attention and to share this dream with others. In particular, I felt I needed to share it with this young girl who had held a large piece of Jason's heart for so many years.

She had loved this mother's son and was now a mother herself. As Jason had represented to me in the dream, Melissa did need all the encouragement and support possible as she embarked upon one of the most important roles of her life - loving and nurturing her own child.

As I struggled with the right words to convey, I recalled those early conversations we had shared after the wreck. She seemed to agonize about "why she had lived when everyone else had died." We could only surmise that God had other plans for her life. This baby was now part of that plan.

I reflected on my promise to Jason to help Melissa as best I could. Nearly a year had passed and it felt as though this letter might be my only chance to reach out to her. I sensed that I was being given an opportunity to honor my promise to Jason. For that, I was extremely grateful. I cried as I sent my letter and prayers to Melissa, hoping that God would use it to encourage her.

I was sorry I never received a direct response from that particular correspondence, but I've learned to always wait on God. His timing is best!

❖❖❖❖❖❖❖❖❖❖

As the anniversary of Jason's death approached, I was overwhelmed with the reality that it had been over a year since I had seen our buddy. I noticed subtle changes in myself. I was no longer shocked to see

*Lifted up from the deep*

photographs of our family with only four in the picture. I was no longer worried about how to answer that ever present question from new acquaintances, "How many children do you have?'' (The answer is still "three," but one lives with God.) I was no longer "scared" of approaching holidays. I had learned to accept God's will in our lives. I had not yet embraced it, but I had accepted it.

Our "year of firsts" was over. We had endured this heartbreak and would continue to do so. God's blessings had strengthened and encouraged us beyond measure. We knew we could depend on His strength throughout the course of all the future years in this tapestry of our lives.

*"for he hath said, I will never leave thee, nor forsake thee."*
Hebrews 13:5

**On this promise, we depend.**

# Chapter 12

# An Overview

As I now reflect upon the many emotions I experienced through the course of that first year without Jason, I am somewhat surprised at my overview. My reaction to the death of one of my children is something I could have never imagined - no parent can. In fact, my friend Cindi reminded me several weeks after Jay's death that we had actually broached this very difficult subject just days before the wreck. We had both agreed at that point in time that we just didn't know how we would recover from such a loss.

Another friend, Jackie, reminded me that to *recover* would mean to "return to the place where we were" prior to the accident. That could never happen. Life as we knew it had changed. That was a fact that we were forced to accept. I don't believe we will ever *get over* the death of Jason. We do, however, continue to *get through* our loss.

I have come to realize that I personally had to face many different emotions in order to *get through* at all. Those emotions would occur when I least expected them and through situations I never anticipated:

> I never expected that I would wake up on many mornings with tear-filled eyes before I was even fully awake to acknowledge my sadness.

> I was surprised at my feelings of despair when I would observe exchanges between other mothers and their sons, or when I would hear a toddler cry for his mother.

> I would feel frustrated - almost angry - when I would see a parent hurriedly dragging a tired, exhausted, crying child through the aisles of a store. I remember an occasion when I was pulling my first toddler through a store as I rushed to get home. Jason had spotted a bright poster laying in a display case. He tugged and pulled at my arm, attempting to slow me down. The little guy desperately wanted to take time to look at the picture. I begrudgingly gave in to his request and we went back to look at the "pretty

picture." The poster that had caught his attention was a picture of bright, colorful, beautiful flowers. He asked me what the words said. The message on the poster was so profound for the situation - "Take time to smell the flowers." It seems that even back then, God was speaking to me through situations in my life, but I failed to recognize them as such. Oh, how I wish I had taken much more time with each of my children to smell every single flower that may have ever caught their eyes.

Maybe that experience so many years ago is what drove me to plant a flower garden in Jason's memory later that year. I feel a surprising comfort when I take the time to appreciate the flowers planted in his memory.

The frantic lifestyles of today can create such seemingly cold and curt relationships with our children as well as with others in our lives. I sometimes feel an urgency to tell others to slow down, take time to treat others well, and cherish every moment they have with their loved ones. We all need to "take time to smell the flowers" - no matter our ages.

- It puzzled me that I spent so much time reminiscing about Jason as a young boy in particular. Every time I would see a dark-headed, brown-eyed toddler, I could hardly contain my emotions. Maybe those emotions echoed a truth that I had come to understand and appreciate more intensely than ever...that no matter how old my children become, they are still mine to nourish and love and treasure. Childhood, in particular, represents such an intimate time in that relationship.

- Likewise, whenever I would see a young man in his twenties, especially with a ball cap worn backwards, my mind would immediately reel me back in time to

*Lifted up from the deep*

remembrances of Jason. I felt a solemn sadness one evening when I saw a group of young, army reservists in a restaurant. They were about Jason's age and I found myself feeling sorry that they were away from their families. I wondered if any of them were lonely, homesick or scared. Those thoughts paralleled the foreboding apprehension and lack of faith that Satan would place in my heart from time to time about Jason's absence from our lives.

- I felt embarrassed when I recognized the envy I experienced as others enjoyed their grandchildren. Guilt filled my heart as I confronted any resentment I harbored about being "cheated" out of that part of our future that would have resulted from Jason's life.

The first year was definitely heavy-laden with an onslaught of emotional baggage. I worried if the load would ever get any easier to carry.

I was almost shocked at the difficulty I experienced in early October when facing Jason's birthday anniversary. I was wrought with much more emotion than I had anticipated. I didn't even know what to pray, but the Holy Spirit knew. He interceded and God answered.

*"Likewise the Spirit also helpeth our infirmities: for we know not what we should pray for as we ought: but the Spirit itself maketh intercession for us with groanings which cannot be uttered. And he that searcheth the hearts knoweth what is the mind of the Spirit, because he maketh intercession for the saints according to the will of God."*
Romans 8:26-27

God then unveiled a special event He had planned in order to make October 8, 1998, an eternally happy day. That event is what I now celebrate every year on Jason's birthday anniversary. The special "happening" was actually planned since the beginning of time, but it came into our view at *just the right time* -

Shortly after Jason died, I noticed that a particular family started attending services at our church. I was told by others that Jay's death had impacted them in such a way that they started looking for their own home church. I thought back to the day of the funeral, hoping that someone - *just one* - would be impacted for God through Jason's death. I was touched that this family seemed to have been affected in this way.

We had been attending a revival in early October. As the anniversary of Jay's 23rd birthday approached, I felt those all-too-familiar waves of hopeless sadness starting to overflow my heart again.

October 8 arrived and I spent much of my day filled with every distraction I could muster. Arriving home that afternoon, I found several cards from friends and family who had taken special care to acknowledge this very sentimental day. Swells of gratitude for their love and support overwhelmed me. My defenses were torn down and my tears soon became a flood. I had not allowed myself to cry so intensely since the earliest days of my grief. I was not emotionally strong enough to attend the last service of the church revival that evening.

I later discovered that this new family to the church had been attending the revival. On October 8, their youngest daughter stepped forward to accept Christ as her Savior. I felt the burden of sadness lift from my heart almost immediately upon hearing the joyous news!

God's timing is an amazing thing...or...

...was this "an accidental sequence of events that appears to have a casual relationship" (the definition of *coincidence,* as defined in the Reader's Digest Illustrated Encyclopedic Dictionary). I believe that it was a *perfectly-timed sequence of events* that have a very *meaningful relationship* - used by God to accomplish His will in different lives.

As Romans 8:26-28 tells us, when the Holy Spirit intercedes for us, he will plead for us in "harmony with God's own will," (from footnotes on Romans 8:26-27 in the Life Application Bible). It is so true that not everything that happens to us in this life is good, but God can use it for good. We need to always ask Him to work things out in our lives and then trust that He will do exactly that - not by coincidence, but by His divine plan!

Jason's death was used to help guide this young girl down a path to a new life of her own. Her pronouncement of that new life on October 8, 1998, was the greatest "birthday gift" I could imagine God might personally share with us as I agonizingly remembered the birth of our oldest son. My anguish was replaced by a joyous event that we could cling to in all future remembrances of October 8. That date was now one of the greatest true "birth dates" in God's record book! It marked the new birth of a young girl who had found her Savior.

The death of our child caused relationships in my life to change. First and foremost, my relationship with God changed significantly. I became so dependent on His mercy that my bond with Him became deeper. For that, I am forever grateful.

From the very onset of our grief, I told Dave that I obviously could not have had Jason without him and I certainly could not have lost Jason without him. Dave was a tower of strength and a fountain of compassion. He allowed me to cry as much as I needed. Often he just put his arms around me, saying nothing. There really was nothing we could say. We both understood each other's loss in ways that no one else on this earth could understand. We respected each other's need to grieve in whatever way was "right" for each other. No matter what the *winds of opinion* might be, we knew the depths of one another's heartache.

My relationships with our other children also grew deeper in ways that I would not think possible. I don't believe it is feasible that I could possibly love my children any more than I did prior to the accident. How does one measure the depths of such love? It seems rather that my relationships with my children became more intense with a profound appreciation for the blessing they are to me.

I definitely know that I am still blessed with <u>three</u> children. Two go to college in Maryville, Missouri, and one lives with God. I truly believe that although Jason belongs to God alone, he is also our child that we will continue to cherish throughout eternity.

I am forever grateful that God spiritually prepared Dave for this trial

*An Overview*

in our lives. Dave remembered the story of Job one evening and shared with me the significance of these verses.

*"There was a man in the land of Uz, whose name was Job...*
*And there were born unto him **seven sons and three daughters.***
*His substance also was seven thousand sheep, and three thousand*
*camels, and five hundred yoke of oxen, and five hundred she asses, a*
*very great household..."*

Job 1: 1-3 (in part)

Job eventually lost all of these blessings and God later restored them *twofold* except, I thought, for the children.

*"So the Lord blessed the latter end of Job more than his beginning:*
*for he had fourteen thousand sheep, and six thousand camels, and a*
*thousand yoke of oxen, and a thousand she asses.*
***He had also seven sons and three daughters."***

Job 42:12-13

As I first studied this story, I couldn't understand why God gave Job only ten more children rather than twenty. With Dave's prayerful guidance, he helped me to understand that the number of Job's children was, in fact, doubled. He only needed ten more children to equal twenty, since Job still had ten children living in heaven with God. The comfort I was given from this understanding of God's Word was nothing less than overwhelming. I had not lost my child - he is waiting at Christ's side to help welcome us to our new home some day.

Today is a time to be grateful
For all God has done in our lives.
And a time to remember not to take anything for granted,
Not a single gift,
Or any person, or even one moment in time.
For when God gives it,
It is precious.                    Author unknown

*Lifted up from the deep*

The precious gifts I have received in my life from God are many and as with many people, I sometimes allow myself to take things for granted. I had certainly allowed myself to take Jason's presence in my life for granted. I naturally assumed that he would always be here and that I would continue to watch his life unfold before me. After all, that's the way we think it's supposed to be in *our* rendering of "the big picture."

Since his death, nearly four years later, I find myself falling back into an old pattern - expecting that each day will pass as usual with those special people in my life remaining in place as always. I am surprised at myself for allowing those assumptions to surface. I certainly know that life can change in the blink of an eye. I suppose that this more relaxed attitude about daily life, however, is an acceptance that "life must go on." I couldn't possibly live my life in a constant state of apprehension.

That very concept that "life goes on" nagged at my heart so very much during the course of that first year. How could that happen when our Jason had died? As we remained in our grief-stricken state and continued to go about the motions of what had become our "new lives," I was confronted with the reality that life *does* go on and that most people would not remain closely by our sides in our "valley of sorrow." It is only natural and expected that others would "get-on" with their individual lives, but at times I felt selfishly abandoned by others.

Most assuredly, however, God never abandoned us. Throughout that devastating time He would always present us with a piece of some friend's heart. When I would feel as though no one except our family was still thinking about Jason, I would get an unexpected phone call or much needed "thinking of you" card. Those gestures were always so welcomed and healing.

I recall the simple, but sincere, words of my friend Debbie who had come to our house to help after the accident. She sounded so apologetic as she recalled the times I had tried to coax her to take the hour-long drive to our house. She was so sorry that this was the first time she had made it up to our home under such difficult circumstances. The important thing was that she was here when I <u>needed</u> her - she allowed her life to be *put on hold* for the sake of my life, and she would do that again today if I needed her to do so. I know that all our friends, like Debbie, would do anything we asked. I know that all our friends grieved deeply for us. Their shared grief and prayers are still priceless to us.

Several friends, in particular, remained "in the trenches" with me. They became a constant reminder to me of what God calls the *fulfillment of His law*.

> *"For all the law is fulfilled in one word, even in this;*
> *Thou shalt love thy neighbour as thyself."*
> Galatians 5: 14

In order to genuinely stay by my side at that time, these friends had to love me enough to endure all phases and degrees of my heartache. They had to share a love with me that would become more important to them than their own peaceful, family existence away from such grief. They had to live Christ's teachings from the Sermon on the Mount:

> *"And whosoever shall compel thee to go a mile,*
> *go with him twain."*
> Matthew 5:41-42

God made sure that His *gifts of friendship* were all in place before He called Jason away from us. In fact, I feel as though the plans of one friend, in particular, were specifically redirected and guided by the Spirit of God Himself!

Jackie had made plans that spring to begin a long week end trip to one of her favorite spots in Branson, Missouri. She had expected to get a very early start on the morning of that trip, scheduled for April 23.

The night of April 22, however, she became very restless and could not settle into a good night's sleep. She later shared with me that the last time she remembered looking at the clock, it was 3:30 in the morning. It was at that point that she was finally able to fall asleep.

Because of her restless night Jackie overslept the next morning and didn't get out-of-town at the *crack of dawn* as she had planned. Instead, she was awakened by a telephone call from my friend Cindi, who had called to tell her of Jason's death.

*Lifted up from the deep*

In all His mighty wisdom, God knew the importance of Jackie's presence in my life at that devastating time. It is so miraculous to me that the Spirit would wrestle with her through the night, but would then allow her to finally fall peacefully asleep at what appears to be the same time that my beloved son departed safely into God's arms - at 3:30 in the morning.

Jackie and I share a very deep friendship that is based on our mutual love of the Lord. She has been a continual source of spiritual strength for me and is my constant prayer partner. God made sure that she remained physically available to me as the *storm* hit me squarely in the face that night. More importantly, He used Jackie as one of His sources of healing to keep me spiritually afloat in my raging sea of grief - a sea that she has ridden with me ever since.

Through every wave of doubt and despair, she allowed herself to be used by God to help calm the storm in my heart. She has helped me to see the shore on the other side and has continually reminded me that Christ is the captain of my ship. Her faith-based claims of survival through this storm were a gift from God for which I am forever grateful. It is a gift that I hope I will never take for granted!...*"For when God gives it, It is precious."*

Another gift from God came in the form of a "surprise package." Marie and I were great college buddies. We had lost contact with one another through the years, but we found ourselves unexpectedly reunited by each other's grief over the deaths of loved ones. Her brother had died suddenly that same spring in 1998.

It seemed like only yesterday that we were carefree college students with our whole lives before us. I recalled so many nights in the dorm when we would gather together with our friends to "solve the problems of the world" and philosophize about "the true meaning of God." We all had our own theories - but they were only theories. We had the rest of our lives to figure it all out!

(It stuns me to think back to my early twenties when I felt as though my life was really just beginning. Jay was the same age as Marie and I when we had determined that "we had our whole lives ahead of us." So did Jason.)

*An Overview*

In Jay's case, however, the rest of his life was practically spent by the time he reached his twenties, but it was still the rest of *his* life! I can never thank God enough for helping Jason to *figure it out* before the rest of his life became his eternity.)

Life had now taken its toll on both Marie and me. Although we lived hundreds of miles apart and had journeyed completely different paths in our individual lives, the subject of God was still on our hearts. In fact that subject was heavy on each of our hearts as we struggled to solve our own intimate problems of our own intimate worlds.

The tone of our discussions had now changed from philosophical babble on "the meaning of it all" to serious acknowledgements of the irrefutable existence of God. Babbling is nothing more than empty discussion that proves fruitless. When I would talk with Marie about the life and death of my son, my faith would become refreshed as I reiterated to her all that God had done for us through our grief. Our discussions proved very fruitful for me and it was my hope that she would feel the same way.

We spent hours on the phone that summer of '98 encouraging each other and listening to each other's hurts. We continue to keep in close touch and wish so often that we understood the reasons for God's decisions.

I am convinced now that if we knew all the reasons for God's design for our lives that our hearts would not be so broken. Rather, our hearts would rejoice in the pure beauty of His plan. *"For when God gives it, It is precious."*

It's easy to embrace God's plans in our lives when we can feel the personal comfort and undeniable blessing from those gifts.

> *"Every good gift and every perfect gift is from above,*
> *and cometh down from the Father of lights,*
> *with who is no variableness, neither shadow of turning."*
> James 1:17

God knew I would need an especially warm and nurturing friend in

*Lifted up from the deep*

my life - someone on whom I could unconditionally depend. He chose someone **He** could rely on for the mission - someone He had blessed with the heart of a servant. God took that compassionate heart and gave it to me in the form of a friend named Cindi.

> *"I therefore,...beseech you that ye walk worthy*
> *of the vocation wherewith ye are called,*
> *with all lowliness and meekness,*
> *with long suffering, forbearing one another in love."*
>
> Ephesians 4: 2-3

I truly believe that Cindi has been given a very important and challenging mission in this life. Anyone who has been blessed to know her would undoubtedly agree that she is the portrait of compassion. God has given her a very important calling and she has answered faithfully and passionately countless times as she extends her tender heart to many. I am so thankful that I have been the recipient of that compassion in my own life.

Cindi allowed herself to truly understand my hurt by allowing herself to *personally* and openly suffer the pain with me. Not only would she listen to me cry, she would weep with me. She would put herself in my place and relate to my suffering from a mother's heart. That is such a vulnerable, tender and difficult place to be; but Cindi was willing to "pay the price" to help me.

As I felt her genuine heartfelt love for my son, I witnessed her own passionate grief surface. She was willing to suffer my affliction deep within her tender heart in order to help mend my broken heart.

Cindi is the personification of what would later become known as the "Jason Simmons Memorial Award" - an award that celebrates the compassionate hearts that God has given to special individuals in our school district. The award is intended to recognize the impact of that gift of compassion when it is used to serve others.

Nothing would make me prouder than to be able to inscribe Cindi's name on our son's memorial award. That is the kind of servant she has been - not a servant to me, but rather a servant to God. It is God who puts Cindi in the lives of others so that they can experience what Christlike love is. I'm so grateful she was willing to be used by God to help me in my gravest hour of need. Her name cannot be engraved on the high school plaque, but it is forever safely and deeply etched in my heart.

*"For when God gives it, It is precious."*

# Chapter 13

# The Rose

I don't recall a reason, but the white rose became a very important and precious symbol to me. I remember a beautiful bouquet of white roses that had been sent to the funeral home. I had taken a single rose from that bouquet to give to the grandmother of the young girl killed in the wreck. It was my way of symbolizing the shared grief that now connected our two families. I also found myself making sure that a white rose was always placed at Jason's gravesite. I was drawn to its beauty, but I did not know why.

In the spring of '99 I was writing to Jenny in her "memory book." The memory book was something I put together for each of my children as they graduated from high school. I started writing to her about our shared experiences in facing Jason's death. I had been struggling with this particular chapter of her book. It was so painful to revisit that time in our lives, but it was impossible to ignore.

Much to my surprise, I started explaining the significance of the white rose. It felt as though I was being guided to write words that were placed on my heart at that exact moment. I was surprised that the words flowed so easily despite the fact that I had never before recognized the reason for the comfort I found in seeing the flower.

I simply wrote to Jenny that for me the rose symbolizes the beauty of Jason's new life in heaven. The color white illustrates the perfect purity that he has received from our Lord. The thorn of the rose characterizes the piercing pain we felt as God called Jason home to Him.

Just as the apostle Paul wrote in 2 Corinthians 12:7 that God had given him "a thorn in the flesh," we felt we had been given a "thorn in our hearts." Paul prayed that the thorn would depart from him. Likewise, we wished that the thorn could be removed from our hearts, but God's response is, *"My grace is sufficient for thee: for my strength is made perfect in weakness"* (2 Corinthians 12:9). The thorn was ours to endure for the rest of our lives.

I later told Dave that I would like to have a white rose bush planted in our yard. Dave planted two bushes along a fence. He also planted a miniature white rose bush in the flower garden that I had planted in Jason's memory. I looked forward to the comfort I was sure we would experience when these roses bloomed someday.

Several weeks later, as the reality of Jenny's graduation grew nearer,

*The Rose*

I found myself slipping into that pit of sadness once again. Although I was proud of Jenny and her many accomplishments, I was selfishly sad to think of her preparing to leave for college. I also had come to the realization that Jason's absence was always more keenly felt at important family events such as a high school graduation.

I foolishly allowed my pain to continue for several days until I finally went to the *Comforter* and fell to my knees. I once again prayed to God for strength to overcome my grief. I asked forgiveness for my weakness and realized how much I needed His strength. I begged for reassurance that Jason is truly okay. I wanted another dove...another rainbow...another sign! I cried myself to sleep while asking God to comfort me and sustain me once again.

The next day was Sunday and I felt reluctant to go to church. I was emotionally exhausted. Any little thing might stir my tears again...*a song...a scripture...a hug*. It wouldn't take much, but going to church that Sunday was "an appointment" I knew I had to keep. How could I plead with God for His help and then choose to stay away from any opportunity to publicly worship Him?

As we sat in the pew, Pastor Dave made a few announcements. Suddenly, I unexpectedly heard him encouraging everyone to come to the Baccalaureate Service the following Sunday. He started explaining that the *Jason Simmons Memorial Award* would be presented at that time.

I immediately fought back tears and found myself haphazardly flipping through the church bulletin as if to distract myself from the beautiful words the pastor was sharing about Jason.

As I became more and more emotionally overwhelmed, I closed my eyes tightly and asked God for strength. I opened my eyes and glanced at the back page of the crumpled bulletin.

There it was...

**- the personal, tailor-made reassurance
for which I had prayed the night before -**

... printed on the back side of a church bulletin:

*Lifted up from the deep*

### The Untroubled Heart

"Let not your heart be troubled"
though storm clouds gather
about,
Rest in the calm assurance
God worketh all things out.

E'en as the night hath hidden,
the work of the thorny rose
Then morning reveals the beauty
and petals unfolded shows.

So, too, for God's saints comes a
morning when, at last, we shall
understand
And thrill to behold the glory,
As wrought by the Savior's hand.

Yes, sometime we'll view
unhindered
what God has seen from the start,
Until then we are given His
promise,
His peace - an untroubled heart!

By Paul Durham

(As appeared in the bulletin published by the Cathedral Press)

It felt as though God had perfectly orchestrated the entire setting. As I gazed through my tears at the picture of the white rose and read a beautiful message of comfort, I was also hearing a man of God fill the church with encouraging words of remembrance for Jason.......

*"...for the Lord hath heard the voice of my weeping.*
*The Lord hath heard my supplication;*
*The Lord will receive my prayers."*

Psalm 6:8-9

*The Rose*

Graduation came and our beautiful daughter made us so very proud. She spoke at the Baccalaureate Service and shared things God had done for her, especially at her greatest time of need. As she gave her testimony to the senior class, it was a blessing to see how God was using Jason's death to strengthen his sister's faith. I thought to myself how privileged Jason would feel to know that his life and death would be used in this way. The first presentation of the *Jason Simmons Memorial Award* was well received. As the recipient was announced, the crowd rose to their feet and the tears flowed from my eyes.

Later that summer, a devastating two-vehicle accident occurred. The drivers of the vehicles were co-workers and each knew the other's family. One driver was killed and the other driver was left with the horror of being involved in an accident that took her colleague's life.

My heart ached for both families. The loss of a husband and father is an obviously painful experience. The burden of the other driver (I'll call her "Sue") was equally on my heart. I shuddered at the thought of how one *split-second moment in time* can reshape a life forever.

While driving to town one evening, I began thinking about that accident and I wondered how the families were coping. I found myself thinking back to Jason's wreck and remembered how grateful I felt that Jason had not made the mistake that caused his accident. I then realized how selfish that relief was...my relief meant it was someone else's burden to endure. Then I thought about Sue and found myself asking God why some people must face such devastating hardships in their lives! Oh God, **WHY**?!

I suddenly felt uncomfortable about questioning God. I quickly grabbed a cassette and turned up the volume as if to drown out my thoughts. As the music started, I realized that it was a tape given to me by my friend Jackie right after Jason died. She told me that she knew I would listen to the music *when the time was right*, but I had never taken the time to listen to it.

As the lyrics to the song rang through the air, I immediately knew that the time **was** right. In fact, the time was **perfect**! The song was full of

*Lifted up from the deep*

llaunting questions that seemed to poignantly answer the very questions on my heart. I pictured a thorny, white rose as I listened to the music.

I was stirred by the recurrence of the imagery of the **white rose** in my heart. Whether it was through the simple placement of the flower at my son's grave; or the words of understanding given to me for my daughter's memory book; or the timely gift of reassurance in a church bulletin...The symbolism of the white rose was something that always brought me comfort. I found myself applying that same imagery to the lyrics of the chorus of this song. The song touched me to the very depth of my heart and its message spoke to the very heart of my questions and doubts: **Why must we suffer thorns in our lives?**

---

## THE BLESSING IN THE THORN

I heard about a Man of God
Who gloried in His weakness
And I wish that I could be
more like Him and less like me
Am I to blame for what I'm not
Or is pain the way God teaches
me to grow?
I need to know

(CHORUS)
When does the thorn become a blessing?
When does the pain become a friend?
When does the weakness make me stronger?
When does my faith make me whole again?
I want to feel His arms around me
In the middle of my raging storm
So that I can see the blessing in the thorn

I've heard it said the strength of Christ
Is perfect in my weakness
And the more that I go through
The more I prove the promise true
His love will go to any length
It reaches even now to where I am
But tell me once again

(REPEAT CHORUS)

Lord, I have to ask You
On the cross You suffered through
Was there a time You ever doubted
What You already knew?

(REPEAT CHORUS)

Words and music by Randy Phillips, Dave Clark and Don Koch

---

*The Rose*

It occurred to me that the message of this song is found in any number of scriptures in the Bible. I had read several passages that teach the importance of suffering, but God allowed His Word to come alive for me through this song and through the imagery of what I considered to be the thorn of a rose.

I had found such comfort in the song and I wanted to share that comfort with Sue. The Bible tells us that God comforts us in order that we might comfort others.

For months I felt a "tugging" at my heart to contact Sue. I wanted to share a few personal thoughts with her. I wanted to tell her about *her song*, but I found myself very reluctant to approach a total stranger about such a very sensitive subject.

I sometimes wonder about that "tugging at my heart." Is it God calling me to do something or is it some selfish need that I'm wanting to fulfill? I've heard others say, "God laid it on my heart." Oftentimes, I wonder how people really know that the thought or message is truly from God.

Was I wanting to contact Sue because "I needed to be needed," or was God directing me to approach her? I felt uncertain about the answer. I listened once again to the lyrics of the song, hoping to find some reassurance about what I should do.....What an awesome thought is expressed in one of the questions toward the end of the song....

**Lord, I have to ask You**
**On the cross You suffered through**
**Was there a time You ever doubted**
**What You already knew?**

The answer to the song's final question is in the Garden of Gethsemane when Jesus fell on his face and prayed, "Father, if Thou be willing, remove this cup from me; *nevertheless not my will, but thine be done.*" Luke 22:42. Even Jesus prayed for direction to honor God's will.

I was immediately reminded to pray for God's will, not mine. I then prayed for patience to wait on God's answer.

The answer came many months later as I was reading a memorial in the paper. It was the one-year anniversary of the death of the man killed in the accident. As I read the memorial, my heart was convicted.

I wrote to Sue and enclosed a recording of "*The Blessing in the*

*Thorn.*" As I mailed the letter, I could only pray that my message would be received in the spirit it was given.

Several weeks later I was blessed to receive letters from both Sue and her daughter. The precious thoughts they shared with me brought such joy and comfort. It is truly amazing how God works! It was as though God said to me, "Comfort Sue and her family with the song and words I give you. In return, I will give them words of comfort to share with you." God didn't actually speak these words to me, but I did feel a personal understanding deep within my heart of His promise, *"They that sow in tears shall reap joy."* Psalms 126:5.

I had been anxious all summer to see the first roses on the bushes Dave had planted the summer before. One of the bushes had died, but the other was full of buds.

I picked the first bloom and brought it into the house. Once again, I felt a special comfort when I looked at the flower. The rose eventually started forming bright red spots on the petals. I was disappointed that the rose seemed to be blemished. It seemed "less than perfect." As I picked more roses throughout the summer, I realized that every flower from this particular bush formed the same bright red spots. **There were no spots on those of the miniature rose bush**. It occurred to me that each spotted rose looked as though someone could have pricked a finger on its thorn and allowed the blood to drop on the petals.

I thought about God's perfect design of a rose. He places thorns for protection on every rose He creates. Could it be that He also places *thorns* in our lives to help protect us from our adversaries by making us ultimately stronger through our suffering?

My mind immediately pictured Christ's crown of thorns that shed his blood. Incredibly, the blood shed from those painful thorns became God's greatest blessing to the entire world!

At that point, I no longer considered my roses to be blemished, but rather felt them to be very special. No matter the cause for the red spots, in my eyes they were uniquely perfect! They were a gentle reminder to me that "the blessing in the thorn" is in the sprinkling of His blood.

*The Rose*

I decided I would take a picture of one of my "special roses." I even thought of sending a picture to Sue for Christmas. I wanted to let her know she was still in our prayers. Although we had still never met, I felt as though she might appreciate the picture of the rose to enhance the imagery of the song.

By now, it was late summer. As I waited for the "perfect rose" for my picture, I discovered that I had waited too long. Many of the roses were not blooming as fully and as beautifully as they had earlier in the season. I decided I would have to wait until next summer to capture that "perfect picture."

I went to bed that evening feeling disappointed that my picture would have to wait. I was worried that the roses might not even bloom next year or that the red spotting on the petals would not occur. I'm sure expert rose enthusiasts would not welcome these spots, but to me they were so unique! So special! Why hadn't I taken a picture when I first saw the spots?

I've discovered since Jason's death that sometimes the smallest disappointments can send me into tears. I always feel so fragile and vulnerable when those feelings engulf me. Here I was again...crying myself to sleep...over a rose bush!

The next morning was met with a beautiful sunrise. I went out to the deck to enjoy the morning air. I was awestruck to discover that our miniature rose bush that had been planted in Jay's memory garden was full of blossoms spotted with red! I quickly grabbed my camera and zoomed in on a rose as closely as I could.

As the tiny rose filled my lens, I was amazed at how this particular rose seemed to perfectly depict the "sprinkling of the blood" that I was wanting to capture. The spots were so symmetrical! The color was so brilliant! The rose was so perfect!

*Thank you, God, for the bug bites...or the timely fungus...*
*or the rainspotting...*
*Or whatever means you chose*
*to leave your fingerprint on our roses. Amen*

*Lifted up from the deep*

The Blessing in the Thorn ....

... Is in the Sprinkling of His Blood

One Saturday just before Christmas, I received a much welcomed phone call from Sue. It seemed at first that we were both a bit uncomfortable with what to say to one another. She told me she had received the picture of the rose and that she felt it was time that we finally met.

We shared heartfelt thoughts and then she told me she felt the need to invite me to her church cantata the following day. She had talked with her husband about it and they both agreed that "they did not believe in coincidences." (Oh, how often Dave and I have discussed the misnomer of the word 'coincidence.')

Sue then explained that at the same time she received my correspondence, she had realized that the church Christmas cantata was entitled "The Winter Rose." She invited us to attend the cantata. It seemed rather providential that we might meet in such a setting.

We accepted Sue's invitation and attended the beautiful musical presentation, which celebrated Christ through the symbolism of the rose. As each song ended, a white rose was carried to the altar and placed in a vase. At the end of the cantata, a single red rose was placed in the middle of all the others, rising above the rest.

*The Rose*

We met Sue and her beautiful family. We hugged and we cried and we silently shared each other's grief. As I left the church, I glanced back once more at the altar full of roses and smiled through my tears:

*"Look around you and see the roses: The friend who is standing with you, The memories of your loved one, The scripture God has given you, The kindnesses others have offered, The work God is doing in your heart. Gather those roses, and let their refreshing aroma fill your life with a confidence that Jesus hears and cares about you..."*

**M.W. Heavilin, from <u>Roses in December</u>**

# Chapter 14

# God's Song Revisited

The *Jason Simmons Memorial Award* was established very soon after Jason's death. Our community had reached out to us in so many endearing ways that we knew we would like to give something back to our community. The direction we would take with the award became evident very early in the planning stages.

Although Jason had been very successful as an athlete in high school and had also received many academic awards, I felt profoundly stirred by the fact that even I, his mother, could not recall how many tackles he made in a season or what his GPA was upon graduation. Those things had seemed so important at the time they were accomplished, but they are not the timeless commemorations that fill up the empty spaces of a broken heart. What was vividly and indelibly etched upon my heart were remembrances of his acts of kindness toward others of all ages.

Our intent in establishing this award, and in presenting it at the Baccalaureate Service in particular, was outlined in the insert that we placed in the Baccalaureate Program:

> In the spring of 1994 our oldest son, Jason, graduated from Excelsior Springs High School. Graduation from high school represented the successful conclusion of an important and precious chapter in Jason's life, as well as the beginning of what we felt would be his long, happy and challenging future. We are sure that many of you here this evening can relate to these same feelings as your children prepare to graduate.
>
> At the time of Jason's graduation we were rather naïve about proper "graduation protocol." Quite frankly, we attended the Baccalaureate Service in 1994 because we thought attendance was required of all graduates. Much to our surprise, that "unrequired service" led us to find our own home church where we were able to grow spiritually together as a family. The importance of that spiritual growth profoundly impacted us more than we could have ever imagined at that time. **Life-changing** decisions soon came to **life-saving** conclusions.
>
> In 1998 our children received Christian baptism.

Three months later our beloved Jason died in an automobile accident. That one life-changing decision (that he chose to publicly acknowledge in January of 1998) immediately became his eternal life-saving gift in April of 1998.

It seems befitting for us to now return to the "garden" of the Baccalaureate Service to sow our own seed in the form of the presentation of the memorial award which has been established in Jason's name. Our intent in offering this award is to recognize the importance of serving others.

In a world that so often promotes the importance of "self," it seems worthwhile to take time to acknowledge the brotherly love and charity we see in others. A charitable person might be described in simple terms as having a *"Warm Heart and Willing Hands."* These simple words are the inscription placed on our son's memorial award.

We believe that a charitable heart is a God-given gift. What a person does with that gift is evidenced in how he lives his life. Jason truly shared his love and compassion with others. We remember and cherish that quality of his character more than any athletic award or academic achievement he earned.

The Ministerial Association has graciously allowed us to include the presentation of the *"Jason Simmons Award"* in tonight's program. We are so grateful for this opportunity. It is truly a special night for our family as we worship together with others in the community, publicly remember our son, and recognize those God-given gifts that students in our high school have chosen to use for others.

We thank those people who took the time to give serious thought to nominating students for this award. We congratulate and thank all students who were nominated for their charitable attitudes and endeavors.

*Lifted up from the deep*

Everyone has special gifts...not everyone can be properly recognized. The important thing is that God is watching and God cares!

We close with the following thoughts by author George Matheson, which take on a very personal significance for us as we forever remember our son...his life...and his death:

"Could it be that we are doing more good than we know? The things we do today - sowing seeds or sharing simple truths of Christ - people will someday refer to as the first things that prompted them to think of Him. For my part, I will be satisfied not to have some great tombstone over my grave, but just to know that common people will gather there once I am gone and say, *'He was a good man, He never performed any miracles, but he told me about Christ, which led me to know Him for myself...'* "

Jason was a good man...He had a *"Warm Heart and Willing Hands"*...Hopefully, through his charitable life, or maybe through his death, he has led someone to think of Christ. That would be his finest legacy.

Our prayers are with each graduating student and every family here. May God be with each of you as you continue your journey through this life. Keep your words gentle, your thoughts generous and your deeds unselfish.

May God Bless You All.

❖ ❖ ❖ ❖ ❖ ❖ ❖ ❖ ❖ ❖

In the spring of 2000, I felt compelled to personally participate in the presentation of the award. It had now been two years since Jason died and I felt strong enough to deal with the emotional turmoil I would face in speaking and singing at the service. I was even more surprised at myself that although the service would fall on a very sentimental day,

*God's Song Revisited*

Mother's Day, I did not shy away from my desire to address the community.

It was rather incredible to me to realize how much God had healed my heart in a year's time. I thought back to the church service of a year ago when I sobbed at the very mention of the *Jason Simmons Memorial Award* by Pastor Dave. Now I was planning on helping with the presentation. There was an overwhelming persistence in my heart to stand in front of the school community that night to express our public appreciation for any acts of kindness that anyone had ever shared with Jason.

I found my heart aching *to do something for* Jason. Intellectually, I knew that there was absolutely nothing I could really *do* for Jason - he would never be in need of anything in his new life. It was I who was in need. I wanted to feel as though I was still nurturing my child in some way. I suppose I felt as though doing something for him would help me feel like a mother to him again. I know that I'm still Jay's mother, but I miss living that role and sharing that relationship.

I decided to speak on behalf of Jason, in a way that might express how his life had been impacted by the actions of others... in ways that *they* might not realize...in ways that *I* might not even realize.

As the time arrived for me to address the crowd that evening, I felt a surprising peace overcome me as I approached the podium. I looked around at the young eyes of the students in front of me who were full of hope and anticipation of *life beyond high school.* I then quickly glanced around the room at the faces of so many parents who were most likely feeling somewhat apprehensive about *letting go* as their children prepared to enter a new phase of their lives. I prayed that my words would be God-given.

As a peace filled me, the words flowed from my heart. My greatest hope was to honor God:

> "Tonight I would like to explain the essence of this award through music. I have chosen to sing a song called Thank You, by Ray Boltz.
> I sing this song and I think of Jason. I also sing this song and dedicate it to all of you who are making a difference

in someone else's life.

"Living our lives in a kind and compassionate way *will* impact others. In fact, there are those in this room tonight whose lives touched our son in ways that they do not even realize. It may have been by the way they endured their own personal challenges or tragedies with dignity and strength and an unshakeable faith. Maybe it was how a coach demonstrated the importance of God in his own life. I fondly remember how Jason's life was so richly blessed by the encouraging words of others and by the Godly lives that others chose to live.

"We feel especially grateful for the words shared by a pastor at the 1994 Baccalaureate Service. Those words helped to lead our son to the Lord.

"When we give to others, God can use those gifts to do wonderful things. We are forever grateful for those many people who impacted Jason's life and his eternity. To you, we also dedicate this song.

"This community has suffered many losses in recent years. Likewise, this community has reached out time and time again to support many broken-hearted people. We must continue to lift each other up in prayer and then let God mend the broken pieces of our hearts.

"Although there is no religious criteria for winning this award, I have chosen this Christian song to explain to you how our family believes we can all influence one another as we walk through this tapestry of life.

"Please remember that 'eternity is truly only one heartbeat away.' Make every heartbeat count.

"To those of you who have learned to share your love with others, we congratulate you. We encourage you. We thank you for giving of your 'Warm Hearts and Willing Hands.'

I concluded by singing the song <u>Thank You</u> which so eloquently thanks those who are willing to give to the Lord by giving of themselves. It celebrates the way that God-honoring acts of kindness can change another's life forever.

As the Baccalaureate Service concluded, our family was gathering to take pictures with the young man who had received the award. Suddenly a man approached me and told me he had been wanting to talk with our family for two years. He then explained that he had come upon the wreck two years earlier and had held our son in his arms and prayed for Jay until the life flight helicopter took him away.

I felt one of the deepest cracks in my heart become suddenly filled with God's love. I quickly found Dave so he could hear this remarkable blessing.

I turned to my friends, Cindi and her husband Gary, who (as always) were there to support us at the Baccalaureate Service. Words spontaneously came out of my mouth with a boldness that surprised me. I hugged them both and blurted out "See what happens when you give to God? He gives so much more back to you!"

I later reflected on those words and concluded that they did, in fact, perfectly describe what had occurred that night. (I say "perfectly" with confidence because I believe they were words placed on my heart by God.) Just as I had found myself surprisingly driven that night to express the importance of giving to the Lord by giving to others, God literally demonstrated that love *back to us* as He revealed the perfect, priceless gift of kindness that He gave Jason the night of the wreck.

The words from a song by Christian recording artist Jim Cole describe my feelings so accurately. In his song called "A Servant's Heart," he speaks of the importance of cherishing every day in this journey of life because we are never guaranteed tomorrow. Through the song he also expresses the truth that none of us can survive this life all by ourselves. We all need each other. We all need to serve each other. We all need to pray for a "servant's heart."

The love that we share with someone today might be the very love that we need tomorrow.

I thought about the many times in Jay's life that he had shared his kind heart with others. I was overcome with gratefulness as I realized that when he needed that love himself - at such a grave point in his life - God remembered our son and made sure he received it.

*Lifted up from the deep*

It seemed uncanny to me that earlier in the evening I had suggested that there were those in the room "whose lives had touched our son in ways that they did not even realize." Obviously, this man who had held our son and prayed for him was someone who had impacted Jason's life in ways that *we* had not even realized. In God's perfect timing, He gave us this information immediately after we had humbly attempted to honor Him in our son's memory. This *gift of knowledge* from God was later described by my sister Leslie as "the greatest Mother's Day gift I could have received - a gift from God."

One of the hardest things for Dave and me to accept the night we got the phone call about the wreck, was that we could not be there to hold our son as he lay broken. The news that God had sent a Christian man to hold and pray for our son in our stead brought us more peace and comfort than I can express.

The horrible thought of the wreck scene was now gloriously replaced by an image of one of God's servants being sent to hold our son. I can now pass the site of the wreck with a visualization of God's merciful gift in my heart. I have since found myself calling that once-dreaded stretch of highway "Jason's Highway to Heaven."

Did this man just *happen by* the night of the accident. Was his presence at the Baccalaureate Service on this particular night just another *coincidence*? Was my burning desire to speak at this specific service in order to thank those who had helped Jason just a *fluke*? So many people today fail to give God the credit to which He alone is entitled. Every time we credit the theory of "happenchance" to situations in our lives, we are in effect discrediting God's sovereignty over our lives.

❖❖❖❖❖❖❖❖❖❖

The Bible teaches that God knows every hair on our heads. He then surely knows every part of my heart - including every crack in its brokenness. Because God is sovereign over our lives, he was in control the night that Jason died. He is control now and He will be in control tomorrow.

As I reflect back upon the beginning of this journey, I remember how

*God's Song Revisited*

God "set the stage" for the drama which was to unfold in our lives through the course of many different "acts." That first "act" began with a song called <u>The Hand of Kindness</u>. (The lyrics are in Chapter 6.)

As God planted that song so deeply and permanently in our hearts, we found ourselves drawing strength off its lyrics time and time again. Not only were the etchings on Jay's headstone and on his memorial award designed to represent God's "hands of kindness," the purpose of the memorial award itself was designed to celebrate the Christlikeness of those who used their own "hands of kindness."

As God gives us ongoing insight for our journey, He frequently brings us back to the lyrics of His song to help put understanding in our hearts.

The song reminds us of the reality of *cause and effect* in this world. (The cause and effect of two cars hitting head-on at 60 miles per hour is somewhat obvious and predictable.) More importantly, the cause and effect of accepting Christ's gift of salvation is sadly not always obvious to some, but it is truly predictable. Accepting His gift or refusing His gift has predictably eternal consequences.

As the song says, (His) *"Forgiveness comes in just a moment, (but) sometimes the consequences last."* In that split moment of time for Jason, the consequences of that accident and the consequences of Christ's forgiveness will last for eternity.

It is the beautiful lyrics of the chorus and title of the song that seems to have come "full circle" to this point of our journey. I had always known that Christ's "hands of kindness" were holding our son. I would often fall asleep at night envisioning Jason being held by Jesus, but I never imagined that God would use someone's earthly hands to literally hold our son on the night of that wreck.

Upon gaining that knowledge two years later, we were able to once again glean deeper understanding of why God chose this song for us to cherish. Because the lyrics are written in first person, it became easy to imagine Jason telling us, *"There's a hand of kindness holding on to me."*

Yes, there **was** a hand of kindness holding on to our son. God used this Christian man's hands to physically hold our son. God then waited until the perfect time to reveal that truth to us - at a time when we would be able to truly comprehend and appreciate the wonder of His gift.

*Lifted up from the deep*

*"For I know the thoughts that I think toward you,*
*saith the Lord,*
*thoughts of peace, and not of evil,*
*to give you an expected end.*
*Then shall ye call upon me,*
*and ye shall go and pray unto me,*
*and I will hearken unto you.*
*And ye shall seek me, and find me,*
*when ye shall search for me with all your heart. "*

Jeremiah 29: 11-13

# Chapter 15

# The Thread that Binds

As the second anniversary of Jay's death approached I soon realized that April 23 fell on the same day as Easter of that particular year. Easter had become another bittersweet occasion on the calendar of our lives.

I was determined to have Easter dinner at our house. My family had all been together at our home for what became Jason's last Easter. Admittedly, I felt some uneasiness in considering hosting the Easter dinner under such circumstances - especially on the very anniversary of Jay's death - but it seemed ridiculous to consider *never* having Easter dinner at our home because of the emotional discomfort it might initially cause.

Just like facing that first Christmas without Jason, Easter at our house with all my family present was an important juncture and a priceless occasion to re-establish.

As we did two years earlier -

- *After church, we all met back at our house for an afternoon of eating and visiting.*

- *We stood in a circle and held hands.*

- *We remembered our loved ones who were no longer with us.*

- *We gave thanks for the many blessings we had.*

- *The line formed quickly for food.*

- *We ate and laughed and shared stories.*

### **Dave and Uncle Larry got out the potato gun.**

Dave had suggested the night before that we should share in a "21-potato-salute" in honor of Jason's memory. I was immediately thrilled with the idea. It was not a flippant or disrespectful suggestion as some might think. On the contrary, it was a very sensitive and personally uplifting suggestion that I thought would perfectly honor and acknowledge Jay's obvious absence on this occasion.

As each family member lined up to shoot a potato through the air in memory of Jason, I thought back to that beautiful "perfect, final memory" that God had given to each of us two years earlier. I thought about Jason's excitement as the pop of the gun sent his *ammunition* flying. I smiled as I remembered the tall-tale of the "potato-lined highway" as described by Melissa and the other girls - a tale that Jason had naïvely accepted as truth.

That reflection further reminded me of one of my fondest wishes for Jason on that Easter two years ago - that he could always keep some of that innocence and naïvety about life. I quietly grasped the reality that those precious qualities about our son were indeed permanently preserved in time as the burdens of this life departed him on April 23, 1998.

As my turn approached to shoot the gun, I became almost weak with emotion...

I took the gun and shot my potato through the air. As I watched the potato soar into the woods, I experienced the excitement demonstrated by my son on our last Sunday afternoon together. I even found myself spontaneously shouting, "AWESOME!"

The *21-potato-salute* helped all of us to confront the undeniable absence we each felt. It allowed us to recall the good times we had enjoyed together. It encouraged us to share our cherished memories of our last day together with Jay.

Leslie remarked later in the afternoon that "a rainbow would really top off the day."

Although we had only our memories of Jason on that day, God blessed us with another special Easter to cherish. Together we shared a priceless gift to remind us once again of God's precious promise of love and continual comfort –

### *The rainbow was back!*

Within minutes of Leslie's spoken prayer, we all went out to the front porch and savored the glory of God's rainbow - another perfectly-timed, glorious grace from God.

Before my brother's death I had failed to deeply appreciate the beauty of the rainbow. I had never given much thought to how Noah must have felt as he rode the waves of that devastating storm. I never imagined how privileged he must have felt to personally receive the glory of God's first revealed rainbow. I never considered the possibility that the comfort and glory of any one rainbow might be for me or my loved ones to personally receive - after all, I would never consider any of us deserving of such a miraculous gift from God.

Because our family has experienced God's sign so often at uniquely perfect times since Chris' and Jason's deaths, I have come to wonder when God creates His rainbow for everyone to relish, if He also places His *bow* in the sky at specific times to encourage some troubled heart(s) somewhere. The rainbow surely encouraged Noah very deeply through his *very personal storm*, even though it was a token of God's covenant for all mankind.

Every time I see a rainbow now, I either feel its healing presence very personally in my own heart or I wonder "for whom God painted this special rainbow." I then pray that whoever needs this particular portrait in the sky will see it and appreciate it for what it is - a personal healing covenant from God.

Recently, after the news of the 9-11 tragedies at the World Trade Center and the Pentagon, I was in solemn prayer at a church communion service. I suddenly found myself thanking God for holding Jason in His arms and removing him from the wickedness of this world. After the communion service, Pastor Randy spoke about the importance of praising God in all things.

This was the first time I was ever able to praise God for calling Jason home - his welfare is already a "done deal." I have since wondered if this powerful prayer experience was symbolic of finally being able to embrace God's will in our lives - an occurrence that I never thought possible because my longing to see and touch Jason is constant.

I have, of course, been in constant prayer that God would shield Jenny and Wes through these uncertain, difficult times. I am saddened that their naïvety and zest for life on this earth have been diminished by the evil they see before them.

I think back to Dave's unknowing preparation for this journey so many years ago. Even then, as he unceasingly studied God's word and searched for that *safe place* to lead his children, God was preparing the many gifts He would give us to fortify our children. It is through the mercy and love of those many gifts that I pray my children (and others) will draw hope and strength throughout the course of their lives.

*"Only take heed to thyself, and keep thy soul diligently, lest thou forget the things which thine eyes have seen, and lest they depart from thy heart all the days of thy life: but teach them thy sons, and thy sons' sons.."*
Deuteronomy 4: 9

It seems that God leads each of us to that *safe place* in different ways and at different times. As confident as I am that God is protecting Jason, I know He likewise has a plan of protection for my other children. Whether it be by holding them in the hollow of His *hands of kindness* or by surrounding them with His angels or by shadowing them under His wings of mercy, His shield of protection is my constant prayer for my children.

❖❖❖❖❖❖❖❖❖❖

I truly believe that God treasures every parent's prayer that is lifted up on behalf of his children.

Just recently I was again reminded of that truth as God listened to my petition for reassurance of Jason's well-being. (I guess a mother never stops worrying about her children - no matter the circumstances.) As I was preparing to leave for work on what would have been Jason's 25th birthday, I was suddenly drawn outside. As my eyes looked up I felt as though God was looking down. Through the glory of those beautiful colors He once again calmed this mother's heart with a rainbow - a beautiful site at sunrise just before I prepared to face an emotionally difficult day. The storm was calmed and the promise was remembered.

I thought back to our first Christmas without Jason and recalled the words in the book Jenny had authored. She had written about rainbows

*Lifted up from the deep*

and simply stated, "God is promising us that no matter what, everything will be all right."

With comforting memories of rainbows filling my heart, I once again reflect on an extraordinary moment of prayer during that solemn communion service. It felt as though God was finally *tying the knot* to one of the darkest threads in the *tapestry* He is weaving in our lives.

That thread has been woven into our lives forever and despite its darkness, it has also become a brilliant, binding cord in our tapestry. It is a special thread that will never become unraveled or frayed because it was used by the divine Weaver to sew His special design into our lives.

Just as Jason's death ripped holes through our lives, God mended those holes with His mercy and love:

> *To every thing there is a season,*
> *and a time to every purpose under the heaven:*
> *...a time to weep, and a time to laugh;*
> *a time to mourn, and a time to dance;*
> *...a time to rend,*
> *and a time to sew;...*
>
> Ecclesiastes 3:1, 4 and 7

# Chapter 16

# Lifted Up from the Deep

It has now been close to two years since I began putting my thoughts on paper. I feel an inexpressible sorrow when I realize that it has been over three years since I have talked to or touched my son.

As strange as it must seem, I also feel an inexpressible joy in the way God has filled our lives. It's as though God has used Jason's absence in our lives to demonstrate His divine presence in our lives. I keep a firm grip on the belief that, for Jason, his absence from us has brought him into the glorious presence of our Lord.

As mentioned earlier, I find myself strangely comforted at times that Jason no longer suffers the injustices of this world.

> *"...and merciful men are taken away, none considering that the righteous is taken away from the evil to come."*
> Isaiah 57:1

Our hope in God's promise makes this grief bearable. Just as our fallen tears became our own personal *pool of grief,* God's continual drops of mercy have rippled through our lives like gentle waves of healing to keep that grief from standing still like stagnant water. He has replaced the bitterness of our tears with the sweetness of His *living water.*

Many times we have wanted to ask God why He chose us to bear such heart-wrenching grief. Likewise, we have wondered why God chose us to receive so many heart-warming mercies. We know that we, like everyone else in this world, are not deserving of such all-consuming love from our Creator.

I reflect back on Dave's prayer the night that Jay died. He prayed that Jay would not become just another statistic. He further prayed that God's will would be done and that God might glorify Himself through Jay's death.

In the hearts of those who knew and loved Jason, he will never become just another statistic. He was a son, a brother, a grandson, a nephew, a cousin, a friend, a best friend, a fraternity brother, a roommate, a student, a fiancé...a **Child of God.**

In our meager attempt to understand our son's death, we feel it was the sole will of God to bring home His child, Jason. His "will was done" on April 23, 1998. We have personally felt the **glory of God** through Jay's death and we now pray that we are honoring God's will by glorifying Him through our words.

It seems very presumptuous to assume that the Great Almighty God would want our help to show others His glory. He certainly doesn't **need** our help! Because we can never really know the mind of God, we can only relate our interpretations of our experiences to the examples we are given in this world:

Dave prayerfully offers the following analogy:

> "When I asked that God would glorify Himself, I did not realize the amount of effort we would have to put forth. Part of the job we have been given is to trust God as we bear the burden before us. The burden, however, is actually being carried by God and is being shared with us.
>
> "Imagine a small boy *helping* his father carry a load. The father could actually carry the load much easier by himself. In fact, the work is oftentimes harder for the dad with the child's *help*. Dad, however, lovingly shares the task with his child for the benefit of his son's development. Through all the effort he could muster, the child did accomplish the task at hand with the *help of his father.*
>
> "If the truth be known, Dad was really doing the carrying while letting only a little of the weight fall on his son's shoulders. The end result is a further understanding of what it takes to follow in Dad's footsteps.
>
> "As we share our encounters with God's mercy we are reminded of a particular verse in the song, *Hand of Kindness.*

> *'And it's hard to walk inside that mercy*
> *When the present is so tied up to the (our) past'*
> (Words and music by Bob Bennett)

*Lifted up from the deep*

"Every day quickly becomes our past. Every deed done and every word spoken also become part of that past, including our compassion for others and our sincere desire that we have not, nor will not, intentionally wound an already injured heart somewhere.

"As we share the gifts God has given our family after Jay died, I can't help but wonder why we were picked to receive such physical signs of love and hope when others may not have been so blessed. I only know that when we asked our Father to glorify Himself that night, He seemed to have responded, *'Sure, but you must help.'* "

❖ ❖ ❖ ❖ ❖ ❖ ❖ ❖ ❖ ❖

Right after Jay died, my sister Leslie shared a thought with me that has remained in my heart ever since. She wondered if the grief we were feeling might minutely compare in some way to the grief God felt as He watched His Son die. I know that I could not bear the grief that God has lovingly placed on Himself.

If, for example, I was all-knowing about other people's reactions to my son's death, I would not be able to endure the following scenarios:

- If people didn't believe that Jason was my son
- If people didn't even care that Jason had died
- If others never recalled Jason's life on this earth
- If friends who said they loved Jason never talked to me about my son

This is the added grief that God must surely bear as so many in this world deny that Christ is His Son...or don't care that His Son died on a cross...or don't take time to recall His Son's life on this earth...or never talk to Him about His Son through prayer.

These constant scenarios must tear at the very heart of God. I could never presume to understand God's grief, but I do wonder if our burden has been destined to bring us to a place that is so beautifully described in that wonderful hymn by Cleland McAffee, *"Near to the Heart of God."*

*Lifted Up From the Deep*

Is it possible that we are like that "small boy" in Dave's analogy? Is our Father really allowing us, His children, to carry part of the burden - not for His sake, but for our own sake?

We now humbly believe that God has allowed us to "carry our part of the load" so that we might better understand how to better "follow in His footsteps." What a hard lesson this has been, but we praise God for teaching us to fear His name.

*"What man is he that feareth the Lord?*
*him shall he teach in the way that he shall choose."*
Psalm 25:12

"With all the effort we can muster," and undoubtedly with our Father's help, we will surely "accomplish the task at hand."

❖❖❖❖❖❖❖❖❖

Although it has been a privilege to write about God's glory, it has also been a difficult task to revisit our son's death in such detail. It would have been easier at times to hide from the reality of those painful memories. To put those agonizing events on paper has removed some of that protective shield that God sometimes gives us in order to cope.

Just as the story of Jonah tells us in the Bible, however, we must always strive to be obedient to God no matter what circumstances we face. In this world of sin, we will all eventually face the depths of stormy waters in our individual lives. We must remember that God will hear us in our suffering:

*"Then Jonah prayed unto the Lord his God out of the fish's belly,*
*And said, I cried by reason of mine affliction unto the Lord, and he*
*heard me; out of the belly of hell cried I, and thou heardest my voice"*
Jonah 2:1-2

Even as Jonah praised God when he was in the whale's belly, we, too, must remain faithful to Him through whatever circumstances He leads us:

*Lifted up from the deep*

> *"The waters compassed me about, even to the soul;*
> *the depth closed me round about,*
> *the weeds were wrapped about my head.*
> *I went down to the bottoms of the mountains;*
> *the earth with her bars was about me for ever:*
> **_yet hast thou brought up my life from corruption,_**
> **_O Lord my God."_**
>
> Jonah 2:5-6

We must obey Him no matter what He asks us to bear in His name. He will save us from our despair. As Jonah faced his own private prison of hopelessness, he "remembered the Lord":

> *"But I will sacrifice unto thee with the voice of thanksgiving;*
> *I will pay that that I have vowed.*
> *Salvation is of the Lord.*
> *And the Lord spake unto the fish,*
> *and it vomited out Jonah upon the dry land."*
>
> Jonah 2:9-10

❖ ❖ ❖ ❖ ❖ ❖ ❖ ❖ ❖ ❖

As I was preparing to conclude this journal about our journey, Dave suddenly found himself writing a poem - something that I have never known him to do before. I feel that his words were given to him as a way to seal our many pages of shared reflection. This poem is our prayer to the Alpha and the Omega of this story:

*Lifted Up From the Deep*

### Belly of the Whale

Make me to make a difference, Lord
Please see that I don't fail
If I flee the task at hand
Set me straight in the belly of a whale.

'Cause I've a head as hard as flint,
And a heart that's way too frail
To say and do what must be done
So it's easy to set sail

Westward when You're pointing East
On a ship and not the trail
Of graceful truth that I should walk
And the effort it entails.

With one more chance to do Your will
Please change my rebel wail
To shouts of joy,  above the shore
Up from that mammal jail.

To blow the horn for all to hear,
That each eye shed his scale,
And turn to look upon the ONE
Who ever fills our grail.

The LORD OF ALL, our CHRIST, our KING,
YAH-SHUA's name we hail!
For He's the GOD WHO SAVES, you see,
From the belly of the whale!

*Lifted up from the deep*

# *Not the end...*
# *but a new beginning*

*"These bodies are only the boxes that we come in..."*

*"The grave is nothing more than our launching pad..."*

**"I will ransom them from the power of the grave..."**
**Hosea 13:14**

*In memory of our precious firstborn son, Jason.*

**A - Corn Publishing**
*2002*

*13566 Little Farm Road*
*Excelsior Springs, Mo 64024*

*Verily, verily, I say unto you. Except a corn of
wheat fall into the ground and die, it abideth
alone: but if it die, it bringeth forth much fruit.*
*John 12:24*